Roses and Broken Sidewalks

My Musical Journey through Life

Cheryl Houck

Trilogy Christian Publishers
A Wholly Owned Subsidiary of Trinity Broadcasting Network
2442 Michelle Drive
Tustin, CA 92780
Copyright © 2023 by Cheryl Houck
All Scripture quotations, unless otherwise noted, taken from THE HOLY BIBLE, NEW INTERNATIONAL VERSION®, NIV® Copyright © 1973, 1978, 1984, 2011 by Biblica, Inc.® Used by permission. All rights reserved worldwide.
Scripture quotations marked nasb are taken from the New American Standard Bible® (NASB), Copyright © 1960, 1962, 1963, 1968, 1971, 1972, 1973, 1975, 1977, 1995 by The Lockman Foundation. Used by permission. www.Lockman.org.
All rights reserved, including the right to reproduce this book or portions thereof in any form whatsoever.
For information, address Trilogy Christian Publishing
Rights Department, 2442 Michelle Drive, Tustin, Ca 92780.
Trilogy Christian Publishing/ TBN and colophon are trademarks of Trinity Broadcasting Network.
For information about special discounts for bulk purchases, please contact Trilogy Christian Publishing.
Manufactured in the United States of America

Trilogy Disclaimer: The views and content expressed in this book are those of the author and may not necessarily reflect the views and doctrine of Trilogy Christian Publishing or the Trinity Broadcasting Network.

10 9 8 7 6 5 4 3 2 1
Library of Congress Cataloging-in-Publication Data is available.
ISBN 979-8-89041-296-6
ISBN 979-8-89041-297-3 (ebook)

Dedication

First of all, the umbrella over the whole manuscript is God. From Him comes the faith, strength, inspiration, and guidance for this book. I trust that as you read it you will feel His peace, presence, and love for all. **A rose.**

My whole heart goes out to my special aunt, Elta Peyton, "Woggie," for the part she played in my ability to come this far in my love for music and the interest in sharing it with the world. I wish she had lived long enough to see and hear all these opportunities that opened up for me over the years. She would have been in the "front row seat" for every one of them. Her gentle, positive, and generous nature and personality shone through to continually encourage me. She provided the way for all the financial obligations (pre-college days) that were necessary to bless me and my dad (her baby brother)! I will always cherish the memories of her engraved on my heart and the memory hand bell stating my appreciation for her love and unwavering faith in me. **A rose.**

Acknowledgments

I would be remiss if I didn't recognize my husband's part in my story. He supported me all through this adventure through prayer, love, patience, late dinners, being a sounding board, and everything in between! God blessed me with the best husband ever!

I want to express my appreciation to all my many friends and especially the most frequent one who encouraged me to share my story. You all had an important part in this coming to fruition.

Thanks, too, to my special friend, Debbie Kindig, for her artistic abilities in helping create the front cover of this book.

Introduction

All dressed up for Easter Sunday service I walked out the door where dad was waiting in the car. I was probably about six years old. The sidewalk was rather old with cracks spreading all over the surface. Right before my eyes was a tiny single flower that had grown between one of those cracks. And it was blooming! What determination that must have taken! **A rose.**

It's my prayer that as I share how God orchestrated many of those "roses" among "broken sidewalks" of my life, it will be an encouragement for you. Never give up. Hold to the hand of the only One who will do the same for you. Hebrews 13:8: "Jesus Christ is the same yesterday and today and forever." May you find hope and faith to watch for the "roses" pushing through your "broken sidewalks."

Over the years there were various close friends with whom I would share occasions of how God intervened on my behalf. Every time I would relate another way God answered prayer they would respond with, "You need to write a book!" My answer was always, "Yeah, right. I don't know how to write a book. And even if I did, I don't have time." As time went on, while sharing my blessings with others, people would mention it again. My reply remained the same. Occasionally, a fragment of those conversations would surface, but nothing that really got my attention.

Finally, an out-of-the-blue conversation with one of the saints in the church seemed to throw a beacon of light on the subject. She began to talk to me about this in a more serious and sincere manner. She suggested that I start, right now, making notes and writing them down in order to be a blessing to other people. "Write the stories now if not for any other reason than to leave them as a legacy for your children's benefit" she said.

Something resonated in my spirit. Half-way into our conversation my attention turned for the first time to the possibility of putting these memories on paper. My brain seemed to be saying, "Yes, let's do this!" My whole attention now turned to God asking Him many questions. *Is this really you, God? Do you want me to compile the miraculous stories of how You have reached out to me with such love and mercy? I don't know how to do this. I neither know anyone who has done this nor where I would start.* My head seemed to be swirling! It finally dawned on me that if this was His will for me I just needed to put it all in His hands and wait for His directions. I did wonder why I had been feeling like there was a certain amount of urgency to get better organized at home and to get caught up with different projects that were still unfinished. It felt as if there was a gentle push behind me toward a goal which I could not define.

In a very few days the Lord began to provide answers.

He reminded me that I did know people who had experience doing this same thing! One was in full-time ministry and offered to pray for God's will, wisdom, and guidance. Another was a friend in church who works in this capacity as a professional writer, and yet another friend who was one of my piano students. "Right under my nose," you might say! They all were so gracious to reach out to me with encouragement, support, and resources. **A rose.**

My Arrival

My parents waited for seven long years hoping for a baby to share their lives. They almost gave up when God suddenly surprised them with my arrival. Life was never the same for them! Even though there were joys present, a "broken sidewalk" was also there. I was fine, but my mother suffered from severe anxiety and clinical depression. It was a successful home delivery, and my dad said I was so tiny he could lay me crossways on the studio couch (we don't hear that term much today) with room to spare! Two of dad's sisters and my grandmother took turns caring for me in the daytime while my dad was at work until my mother was able to recover and take over the responsibilities. **A rose.**

0-2 Years

Early in life, music caught my attention. My mother related that she often listened to her Lutheran pastor on the radio. All through the sermon I would sit on the floor and quietly play with my toys. The minute the choir started to sing, I would stop playing and rivet my attention on their singing and start to silently cry. Tears would quietly form little rivulets on my face until the music stopped and I returned to my toys. Since I wasn't talking yet, she was concerned about my behavior, thinking music disturbed me. She discussed it with her pastor only to find out that one of his daughters experienced the same response to music. He told my mother that evidently when I became older I would be working in some capacity of music ministry.

> *"For I know the plans I have for you, declares the Lord, plans for welfare and not for evil, to give you hope and a future" (Jeremiah 29:11).*

3-5 years

Music caught my attention again. My mother shared with me that I was sitting on her lap in church one Sunday morning listening to the choir sing. I watched their faces intently and suddenly slid off her lap before she could intervene. Running down the aisle, I loudly exclaimed, "There's my goggy!" Evidently I couldn't or wouldn't say "daddy." I swiftly continued up the aisle and crawled up into the choir loft. Reaching my goal, I was swooped up into my daddy's arms and promptly returned to my mother's lap. Needless to say, the congregation chuckled over the incident, much to my mother's chagrin, and the choir probably missed a few notes, but I found my idol! By the way, I had improvised with my own language using "goggy" for daddy! Later on, my favorite aunt's name became "Woggie." Only hers remained so the rest of her life.

Country life

I was about five years old when my parents moved out of town to the country. Everything was so exciting to me. I found new and different things every day. There was my shepherd dog which followed me every step I went. Then there was the pet chicken that I fed and watered until it also followed me around! But my favorite thing was a miniature clothesline that dad created for me. It was just like mom's, complete with my very own clothespins and sackcloth holder. Of course it was a lot closer to the ground so I could reach it. On washday I would get all my dolls' clothes and proudly pin them on my little clothesline!

Life was good! All except the time when I walked to the back porch and started walking up the steps only to find something stretched all the way across the porch. Too afraid to go closer to what looked like a monster I turned around and ran back to dad. " Dad," I exclaimed! "Come quick; there is a great big worm on the back porch!" With an excellently aimed shot the huge snake became history.

Fired!

For a while dad had no car to drive into town to his job. So he shared rides with a friend. Our house stood on a hill away from the country road below. Every morning dad walked down the hill to meet his ride. Every evening when it was time for him to come home I and my dog would walk down to the road and wait for him to arrive and escort him up the hill to the house. One day as we walked up the hill he told me he had been fired. I had never heard that phrase before. My mind became very busy conjuring all kinds of pictures. I pictured him walking around a fire perhaps. He didn't appear to be in pain, so I concluded that probably wasn't what happened. I don't remember if he tried to explain what it meant, but then I might have been too busy mentally trying to figure it out by myself. The next thing that I remember happening was packing up all our things and moving back into town. He had found a new job. I remember missing those walks, including the little creek under the bridge where I saw flowers and sometimes a frog.

My dad often demonstrated his musical ability on violin, mandolin, and anything else that had strings for me to enjoy. His face would light up when he picked up his instrument. He loved to play for one person or for a hundred, it made no difference!

Betsy Wetsy Doll

While living in the country dad would often spend many weekends playing violin music for house-raisings and barn dances, etc. The German community helped everybody in big projects, such as building a new house, barn, or just enjoying weekend entertainment. I was too little to go along and was very teary-eyed every time he left. One evening he pulled me up in his lap and told me if I didn't cry he would get the Sears and Roebuck catalog out the next morning and I could pick out a new doll. I still have that Betsy Wetsy Doll. She was the first doll that actually took a bottle and wet its diaper! Now, seventy-seven years later, I still have that doll!

Dangerous Bridge

It's amazing how young a person can develop a fear of something. All my life I have been fearful of water. There wasn't anything that I could identify as the cause. As I began reviewing material for this book a mental picture popped up. My mother and I were on our way to town. The route we normally took included crossing a creek that often flooded its banks. Mom heard the bridge was out, but she said we would start and go as far as we could. Maybe it was back in business. I can still see myself standing in the back with my arms folded over the front seat intently watching the road ahead. The closer we got to the bridge, the more frightened I became. I began to beg her to slow down, just stop, or better still turn around and go back home. About that time we saw a car coming toward us. As we were even with each other the driver rolled down her window and told mom the bridge had been cleared and was ready again for traffic. It took the rest of the way to the bridge for me to relax and process the fact that since the other car got over the bridge and made it safely to us, it is just as safe for us to continue forward. I still can recreate that feeling of fear of our car rolling into the water. God is slowly helping me to release that fear. Today I have to admit I never got close enough to water to learn how to swim. I would do it if I didn't have to get wet! You would probably see me yet today close my eyes as my husband drives over a body of water! **A broken sidewalk.**

Foot Injury

Dad's musical ability came at a price. When he was a young man he worked all summer in the fields as a farmhand until he earned a few meager dollars and bought a used violin from one of the farmers. He had an uncle who directed a band and would have taught him, but there wasn't enough money to pay for the lessons or to travel to where he lived. So when the farming season ended, he tried to discover all by himself what made these strings talk. One day his father asked him to go outside and chop some wood for the wood stove. Reluctantly he went out, but when he slung the ax he missed the log and it landed on his foot. He lived too far out for the doctor come to him, so he moved into town where his older sister and husband lived. They owned a funeral home there and it was close to the doctor. All winter long he laid in bed with that violin squeaking and squawking until he mastered what he heard in his head. When I was older it was this ability that encouraged me to continue pursuing music. **A rose.**

Stage Fright - 5 years old

I learned my first song to sing at age five, and dad accompanied me at church with his mandolin. The only problem was when I got to the platform and I looked out, there seemed to be way too many people to remember the song or even the title! Nothing came out of my mouth! That fear of speaking followed me all through my high school years. **A broken sidewalk.**

Piano Lessons

Aunt Woggie, the older sister of my dad, decided that it was time for me to learn how to play the piano. Again my folks didn't have enough extra money to buy a piano. **A concrete wall.** Nevertheless, my aunt found a used one, paid for it, had it delivered to our home, and found a teacher. Not only did she provide the piano, teacher, and lessons, but several years later an accordion as well and all the lessons and required books for nine years! My music education has started. **A rose.**

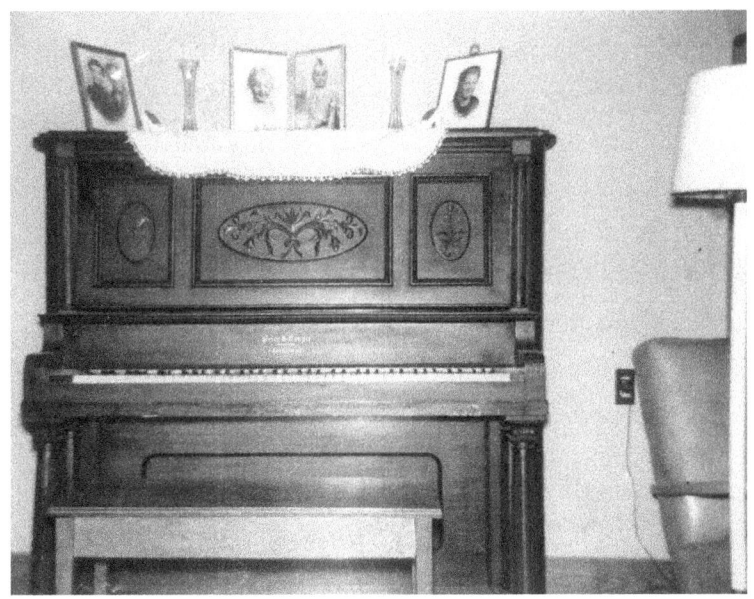

Miracle Dolls - 6 Years old

Listening in Sunday School class gave me an early, child-like faith that whatever was said about God doing miracles was real! There was a period of time when every night before getting tucked in for bed that I would go to the playroom where my dolls and toys were kept. Tucking all four of my dolls in bed, I said to God, "Now when I wake up in the morning I am expecting You to have turned these dolls into real babies so I can have someone to play with" (my parents never blessed me with any other brothers or sisters). Of course it didn't ever happen. Each morning I would hurry back to the playroom, fully expecting to see real babies waiting for their morning bottles! Not to be daunted I repeated this routine every day until it slowly faded as I grew older. **A concrete wall?** Years later when my husband and I joyously received our fourth child, God reminded me of my child-like prayer. "I heard your prayer and never forgot you. Here is your petition granted!" God's calendar is not the same calendar as ours. He is so faithful and always on time! Maybe 11:59 pm, but still on time. **Another rose.**

Watering The Pie?

When my mother was feeling well she loved to bake. Her finished products were so yummy. Just like bakery goods. One day as she was preparing to bake a cherry pie I was sitting at the table watching as she prepared the homemade pie dough. Before she placed the top cover of the piecrust onto the bottom crust she would dip a spoon in water and moisten the edge of the bottom crust. That would help seal the two crusts together to prevent seepage of cherry juice through the opening. Otherwise, it always managed to drain into the bottom of the oven and smoke up the kitchen. She shared with me years later that I asked her, "Mommy, what's you doin'? Watering the pie?"

Bedtime Treat

While we are talking about food, what a sandwich she could make! At night she would tuck me in and listen to my prayers. "Now it's time to go to sleep," she would say. I would let her almost get out of the room and call out, "Mom." She knew what was coming. "What do you want?" she would ask. "I am hungry." She always asked what I wanted to eat, knowing what I was going to say. "I want a sandwich with peanut butter, syrup, catsup, mustard, and mayonnaise." The first time I asked for it I was joking about the horrible combinations, expecting a resounding denial. To my surprise she said "Ok." *Oh my*, I wondered, *What in the world is it going to taste like?* She produced my sandwich probably thinking I wouldn't be able to get past the first couple of bites. To my surprise it wasn't too bad. It became a ritual for quite a long time and I lived to tell the story! Only a loving mother would do that. **A rose.**

Gift of Salvation

My mother was a Pentecostal lay preacher, but as I mentioned earlier she suffered nervous breakdowns at regular intervals. I vaguely remember her teaching Sunday School in the Primary Class that I attended. So I learned many Bible stories during her good times.

During one of her difficult times, my best girlfriend's mother picked me up to go to church on a Sunday night. This friend and I sat next to her mother throughout the whole sermon whispering quietly and scribbling pictures in our children's bibles. I can't remember anything the pastor preached about that night. At the end, he asked everyone to stand and gave an invitation for anyone who wanted to experience God's forgiveness to come forward. Suddenly, I felt like there was such a heavy weight on my shoulders. So heavy that I knew instantly I had to walk up there. I couldn't explain it, but I instantly knew I had to respond. I turned to my friend and asked her if she wanted to go with me. She looked rather surprised, but agreed to go. As soon as I reached the altar there was a sweet Christian lady ready to kneel with me and explain what all this was and what it meant. After repeating the sinner's prayer it felt like a ton of weight had been lifted off my shoulders! The lights seemed brighter and I felt as light as a feather! She explained that the next step was to be baptized. I immediately asked if I could do it that night! Later, I got to do it when the opportunity opened. **A rose.**

Discouraging Testimonies

My dad picked me up after church. I was so excited to tell him what happened to me at church. He seemed unable to process this news and didn't really know how to respond. It was a little disappointing, but I knew my mom would be excited about it when I got home. And I was right. She told me she was proud of me and glad that I was now a Christian. The next day I couldn't wait to get to school to share my good news! My teacher's response was, "What did you say?!" "Oh, okay." I was surprised at her not being very supportive. I thought everyone would be as happy as I felt. **A concrete wall again.**

We had moved into a duplex and the other couple were friends of my parents, both couples having moved there from the German community and attending the same Lutheran church. Dad thought that this would be helpful because my mom was back in bed again for probably several months or more, never getting up except to eat a little or use the restroom. I was only six years old and didn't know how to cook for myself while he was at work. My mother did manage to explain to me from her bed how to iron. Slowly, I graduated from ironing dad's handkerchiefs to pillow-slips and eventually my dress so I wouldn't have to go to school in a wrinkled dress.

The lady in the other half of the duplex would occasionally bring over a pot of vegetable soup or brownies, etc. **Another rose!** After excitingly sharing my story with her, she replied with, "Oh, that is nice, honey. Let's go into the kitchen and get some cookies." By now my enthusiasm was beginning to wane. Was there anyone who was excited like me and would like to know what happened that made me feel so wonderful?

I returned to our half of the building and decided what I was going to do. I knew her pastor was planning on visiting her the next day. I said, "Mom, when the pastor comes to visit you tomorrow, you tell him what happened to me last night, but I am going to crawl under the bed in case I get disappointed again!" Obviously, this time was different! He was quite amused about my plan but encouraged me to grow with that tenacity to learn more and more about serving God. **Another rose!**

Don't Throw Rocks!

My dad was looking for a different job and was talking to a friend who sold Ford tractors. Dad would occasionally stop by this friend's house. A few times he would take me with him to play with this friend's daughter, who was my age, about six years old. I always looked forward to these visits. If I were lucky she would ask her mother if we could have some Spearmint gum. The girl and I would divide the sticks and play outside in the back yard. A little boy next door would come over and end up throwing rocks at us. I wasn't used to anyone being so mean. I remember thinking, "Does he understand that he might throw a rock and put out our eyes?" I asked him to come and sit down with us. I wanted to tell him something. He looked rather dubious but I told him it was okay, I just wanted to talk to him. "Please shut your eyes," I said, "Now do you see anything? Do you know that when you throw a rock at someone it might hit their eye and damage their ability to ever see again?" I didn't know that my friend's mother was listening from the kitchen window in the house. When my dad started to leave she told him she had been listening his little "teacher" daughter. Perhaps a taste of my desire to be that teacher years later.

Let's Play Store

By the time I was in first grade I was finding excitement in working with addition and subtraction using money. Every evening I would look forward to dad coming home from work. That is when he would play grocery store with me. When I heard the car come into our driveway I would first race to hide under the covers (mom's bed had been placed in the living room next to the kitchen). I pretended to be hiding and it was part of the game for dad to find me! After a few futile attempts I couldn't wait any longer so I would throw over the covers to tell him, "Haha, you couldn't find me! Let's play store!"

He would pull up a kitchen chair in front of his. He would pull some change out of his pocket and the game would begin. "I want to buy a loaf of bread. Here is a dollar, I don't have the exact amount of money. How much will I get back?" Back then there weren't cash registers that rang up the price and told you how much change the customer would receive. He taught me how to count from the cost of the bread with pennies, nickels, or quarters until I got to the dollar bill. Little did I know how much this game would eventually blossom into being involved in different business ventures. **A rose.**

Dad would have been an excellent school teacher. Looking back on these activities, I thought he took me sometimes for the boy he never had. He proceeded to explain how and why pistons moved up and down in the car's motor. How electricity worked. Telephone wires had a bundle of electrical colored wires, blue, orange, green, brown, slate. And in that order. He even set up pistol target practice with me out in the country at Aunt Woggie's house. He claims I got very accurate with my aim, but I am sure it didn't last too long. I probably couldn't hit the side of a barn now! There was one thing that never surfaced in explanations, and that was how to change a tire. I am actually kind of glad. It always looked like a dirty job. He exhibited teaching abilities just like one of his sisters who helped him through eighth-grade and helped me in my senior year of high school. **A rose.**

Looking back to his cheerful participation in what would seem like just a little girl's fun game reminds me of our Master. How closely He is concerned with our day-to-day activities, heart's desires, and provisions. He loves us more than you can ever count coins! **A rose.**

"For God so loved the world, that He gave His only begotten son, that whoever believes in Him should not perish, but have eternal life" (John 3:16, NASB). **A rose.**

Revenge Time!

I must have inherited a tiny streak of feisty defiance from my mom's childhood. In the first and second grades I dreaded recess. Everyone had to go out to the playground. All grades, first through fifth, were together and I didn't feel safe from the older students anywhere except staying on the merry-go-round. The upper grades were so much bigger than I. Add to the fact that there were two boys who went around bullying other students. They even tried to make the merry-go-round go way too fast for my comfort. I waited and watched until those two boys were sitting down at the top of the slope of our playground. Their backs were turned to me. Suddenly, I knew what I thought they deserved. I got off the merry-go-round, ran toward them, and gave both of them a sudden push on their backs. Down they both went, the duo rolling down the hill. The bell rang and I was smugly smiling. I was surprised at my courage to teach them a lesson. After getting back in class, panic struck! What if they find out who did it, and knew I walked home many blocks by myself? Repentance came swiftly on my part! I promised God I wouldn't ever do that again if He kept me safe on my walk home! Now trying to bargain with God! God's mercy and protection promises prevailed! **A wilted rose?**

Moving Again

Dad had recurring bouts with extreme asthma until one day the doctor told him he either had to find another job away from roofing shingle materials or get his life in order. God blessed him with a job which answered the doctor's advice. After telling my first two years of school goodbye in Vandalia, Illinois, dad moved us to Vernon, a small rural community of farming. Here he could enjoy the outdoors while driving a tractor for the owner of multiple acres. I even got some experience driving the tractor while sitting on his lap. That farm owner also sold new Ford tractors, and it was part of dad's job to deliver them to the buyer's home. His boss bought miniature models of the Ford tractor to give as gifts. Yes, I received one of those, too! Still have it displayed today on a shelf with my Betsy Wetsy doll. **A rose.**

Chasing Mumps

Oh, how different this town was! Everybody knew everybody. Classes were very small and it felt like family to me. The only problem with this close environment living was when one student contracted a virus or childhood disease, most of the other classmates got to share it! I experienced all but the mumps. Feeling so terribly left out I told my mom one day that I was going to go visit my friend from class. This friend was home from school because of having mumps, but I didn't bother to tell mom that. When I arrived at my sick friend's house her mother warned me about her daughter being sick with the mumps. I told her, "That's ok. My mom knows I am over here." In my mind I told myself, *I'm not lying, mom does know where I went.* I visited with my friend, laughing and talking as long as I could possibly stay. When I left I was thinking, *Now, that was surely long enough for me to catch them, too.* Several days went by, but no mumps. I was so disappointed. My

Guardian Angel was looking after me, I guess. Acting in His wisdom He figured that the disgrace of not being able to contract mumps was enough punishment. I never told mom for years!

Business Venture

Living in Vernon brought other new experiences. I stepped up a notch in the business world. Now my vast knowledge of money practice from the play store game had been lying on the shelf for a while. Dad couldn't find rental houses soon enough to start working there. So he bought a trailer and got permission to park it beside a tiny grocery/restaurant as long as he paid them for the electricity we used. The owners were grandparents and started finding activities for this little girl of seven. The grandmother was sacking dry beans in small white sacks and placing them on a scale to weigh one pound. Then she taped it shut. One day she invited me to help her. I was so excited. For my wages I could reach into one of the cookie bins and take two cookies of my choice. Back then cookies were sold in bulk rather than in packages.

Meanwhile, dad had been working out on many acres of farmland and was evidently unaware of my recent "employment." Mom sent him to the store to get some things, and of course I had to tag along. While he gathered his grocery items, I naturally headed for the cookie bins and helped myself. Oh my goodness! You would have thought that it was prison-worthy! Thanks to the grandmother who saved my character. She explained that I had been given permission to do that because I was working there sacking beans for her. Dad had almost cooled down by the time we walked back to our trailer. Nevertheless, the business world appealed a little more to me. I didn't know how much later this would be helpful in our own Bible Book store. Wonder what else I could learn? **A rose.**

Later on, when mom was feeling better, she ordered some greeting cards and wall plaques delivered to our house. She surprised me with them saying, "Now you can make some spending money. These are yours to sell door-to-door." I had never sold anything before, but everyone knew us, so they bought from me to help me. The first shipment sold out quickly. A second one also sold. I was getting excited about this selling idea. I didn't realize how this was increasing my social skills with meeting people, having to explain what I had, and making change again!

In the summer I decided I wanted to pick strawberries for the owner of a large patch. He was advertising for help and dad said, "Why don't you help pick for him?" At a huge five cents per quart I made enough money to buy my first Minnie Mouse watch. That was the best looking watch I had ever seen. Confidence was building! Two more opportunities presented themselves and I added babysitting and fixing a light Saturday night supper meal for an older couple who lived next door. **A rose.**

But back to the music interest my family was promoting. Pianos don't fit very well in a trailer. I felt like I was living in a doll house and was having fun pretending. The piano had moved with us but was stored until we found a house. The grandmother at the grocery store suggested I practice at her daughter's house. She had a piano and lived just across the street. God always provides. So back I go to daily piano practice at her house. It didn't last long. I felt so intimidated being there because it seemed like the whole world was listening to me. My practice slacked off quickly. One day mom told me, "If you aren't going to practice, we are going to tell your Aunt Woggie (yes, her strange name still stuck) to stop paying for your lessons. She is wasting her money." My response - "Okay, that's fine with me." So I thought.

Time was quickly moving along. I had come from Vandalia completing grades one and two, having to walk for blocks and blocks by myself every day to attend school. I even had to go across a railroad crossing. Thinking back on that now sends shivers down my spine. Six years old and all the possibilities of being run over by a car or hit by a train. God had surely placed a hedge of protection around me. Now in Vernon I finished grades three through six. It was so convenient in that I only had to walk one block each way and each day. **A rose.**

God Fills In the Gaps

When I look back over my shoulder throughout these early years it appears that I spent much of that portion of my life in a quiet environment by myself. However, at the time I wasn't aware of feeling lonely. There wasn't any other time with which to compare. I didn't have any brothers or sisters and my mom was sick much of the time. She couldn't spend a lot of time entertaining me or teaching me age-appropriate activities. Dad was gone during the daytime at work.

At the time I didn't worry about what was going on or lament about nothing to do because I didn't experience a feeling of loneliness or being bored. God was filling in the gaps. I played house with dolls. Remember the pet chicken and a dog I had when I lived in the country? Later I had a beautiful yellow Persian cat, at least until the day mom took me to the dentist. She didn't know it had slipped out the door. Unfortunately, after returning from the dentist it never came back home. Goldfish in clear glass bowls decorated my room more than once.

Grandma's Kitchen Nursery

I always looked forward to going to one of my grandmother's houses because I never knew what exciting animal might be there, ready to eat from my hand. Living in the country, she usually had baby chickens, kittens, piglet, and once a baby lamb. If one of these baby animals was rejected from its mother or became injured, grandma would bring it into the house for restoration. It would be placed in a big box with warm rags for blankets behind an old-fashioned cook stove. That served as a nursery until the baby animal grew big enough to join its animal family. I would get to hand feed them with a large baby bottle right there in the warm kitchen.

She had cows so fresh milk was always available. Along with fresh milk came thick cream. She cooled crocks of the milk topped with that cream in her cellar. Sometimes in the kitchen refrigerator. That is the first place where I rushed trying to scoop the cream off the milk and eat it with a spoon before I got caught! Fresh butter and homemade cottage cheese were also the best ever. I can still smell the aroma of homemade bread. Then to top it all off she would take the bread and spread it with the rich cream, spoon brown sugar on the top, and place it in the cookstove oven until it browned on top. Ooh, ooh! Yummy!

Grandma also introduced me to growing different kinds of flowers in self-dug beds. She would share seeds and flower bulbs for outdoor beauty. She even had flowers in her living room sitting on top of her pedal-type Singer Sewing Machine. She prided herself with growing many varieties of African violets. She taught me their names and how to grow them from starts. To this day I have five varieties of different colors blooming profusely in my spare bedroom. Every time those violets are ready for a drink I think of grandma and her Singer Sewing Machine in front of the window. **A rose.**

My other grandmother also lived in the country. She and another aunt lived with my Aunt Woggie. This aunt would take me for long walks on country roads. There were very few cars. While walking she would point out wild flowers and teach me their names. My first flower that I learned was Queen Ann's Lace. Next, I fell in love with bluebells growing along a little stream of water. As different birds sang out she would tell me what kind of bird sang that particular song. Even the trees can be identified by their bark. So she loved God's nature and took the time to share it with me. I have so much to be thankful for with both grandmas and Aunt Woggie who God used to fill in times of my young life. Life without them could have changed my perspective forever. This reminds me a portion of Proverbs 18:24 that says "…there is a friend who sticks closer than a brother" (NIV). And that friend is Jesus. **A rose.**

Beautiful Wardrobe

During those summers God gifted me with another work of heart from, yes, Aunt Woggie. She was an art teacher who used those free summers sewing a complete wardrobe for me to wear each school year for seven years. Adding to that she ordered me a new coat and new shoes every fall. For a while even a new doll came with it. By my seventh-grade year I was spending Saturdays learning from her how to sew for myself. Since then I continued sewing new clothes and enjoying a new skill all the way to creating my own wedding dress. At some point I understood that she had taken me under her wing as the little girl she never had. God is so good! **A rose.**

Lessons Resumed

A year from declaring I was done with the piano I suddenly realized that I was missing it. I asked mom if she would ask Aunt Woggie if I could resume lessons. Of course, I promised from the bottom of my heart I would practice faithfully. As you probably guessed, my aunt had been patiently waiting to hear this good news.

This time the piano seemed to be a magnet drawing me to it. It became my escape from times of stress and questions, to an adventure into peace and tranquility. Hardly could I walk by without stopping to sit down and playing something. It might not always be my lesson material but no longer was it a chore. Mom always said she could tell what mood I was in by the way I played. I might start out with strong percussive notes until I began to relax into a smoother, gentle style.

The Lightbulb Turns On

As months went on I was struggling with what I was learning and what I was hearing in my head. Dad was helping me with playing by ear by using a simple chording structure, and I was a fledgling piano instructor going for weekly classical lessons, but that improvisational method and classical method didn't seem to mesh together. I played, cried, and prayed. Played, cried, and prayed. **A broken sidewalk.**

    I will never forget the day when the light bulb turned on. One Sunday afternoon I was practicing the hymn of the week (mom insisted on a hymn every lesson). It was the song, "Come and Dine." Something seemed to say, "Read your music vertically instead of horizontally." I stopped playing and looked at the music. My eyes were drawn to the bass clef (left hand notes). I recognized the letter names of the notes and continued to look upward through the tenor note, on to the alto note (right hand notes) and the soprano line. To my utter amazement those four notes spelled a chord! Was I on to something? My heart started beating faster! Silently reading on, I saw the chord structure that was always there under the surface, so to speak. God finally broke the mystery open that I had been looking for a long time. Now I understood how people meshed the two worlds together - reading the music and adding the improvisational chord structure together. Many hours later found me checking out hymn after hymn. A whole new world was now open for me to explore. I wouldn't have traded that experience for a thousand dollars. **A rose.**

Fledgling Piano Instructor

One afternoon a friend in town asked me if I would teach her little girl how to play the piano. Sounded shocking to me. Me, teach somebody else? I don't know how to teach piano! I had graduated to playing piano for my church on Wednesday night, Sunday night, and finally Sunday morning but had never tried to teach anyone. After thinking about it a long time I thought, *Well, why not? I can at least just show her some simple things.* And I still had my old beginner books. Plus, she was too young to argue with me about anything I would be telling her. I didn't know at the time that when you are teaching others you learn more sometimes in the process than they do. God was working His plan for my life. How could I have ever known the joy and satisfaction of helping others experience the reward of having music in their life! My life was opening up to a whole new chapter. Going down the road which would result in teaching many students a week, becoming an avocation, career, and much more to come! Sh-h-h, don't tell anybody yet, but it also played a part in meeting my future prince charming. **A rose.**

Learning A New Instrument

My mom began to feel left out of the music circle. I was learning piano and dad played violin and many other string instruments. So she began asking me questions about reading music and decided she was going to venture out. She wanted to try something different from what my dad and I played. So she drove to Staff Music House in Vandalia and signed up for 12 free lessons with the purchase of a 12-bass accordion. The right hand keys were white and black just like my piano, so she thought how hard could it be to learn those little red buttons for the left hand? After about three lessons I began to notice that time between lessons was pushing out further and further. Eventually, she decided that she wasn't interested anyway and would have missed out on the remaining free lessons. I was studying it one day and thought, *Why can't I learn to play it?*

    I already knew how to play the right hand. The left hand buttons were the same as the chords dad was teaching me in ear training. Mom called the music store and asked them if I could come to take the rest of the lessons. I loved the challenge of something different and looked forward to taking the lessons. After they were completed I began working on combining the information coming from my piano lessons and the ability of ear playing from my dad. God was laying another part of preparation for what He was calling me to do. In an earlier section of this story I mentioned the fact that Aunt Woggie had been watching my interest in the accordion and secretly ordered a 120 bass accordion to be shipped to my house. **A rose.**

Wagon To The Rescue

Dad found a second house that was larger and right across from a larger grocery store. He sold our trailer and moved the piano out of storage. The house was on the same street as the first house. I got impatient with getting things moved, so I took the matter in my own hands. At least for my things. I rounded up a friend to help. She and I would carry a drawer at a time from my bedroom upstairs, put it on my little wagon and pull it down the sidewalk to the new house. It didn't take very many trips until my friend decided this wasn't fun anymore and went home. It's so hard finding good help!

Men And Guns

After living in this larger house for some time two men knocked at our back door. We had an enclosed porch where our washing machine and rinse tubs were. There was a screen door for the first entry before the main door to the kitchen. My mom had gone to visit a friend so only my dad and I were home. My bedroom was off the kitchen so I heard them knock and yelled to dad, "Someone is at the door." He cautiously opened the kitchen door and found the men already on our porch. One was on crutches and the other one was doing the talking. Dad didn't recognize either of them. Which sent up red flags because Vernon was so small everybody knew everybody and their dogs. We didn't know either of them. Dad's mind went to the thought that they might know he is the manager of the lumber yard. This means that since Vernon didn't have a bank it caused him to have to bring the money home with him every evening. The man kept repeating, "We just want to talk with you, sir," as they kept encroaching across the porch to him.

I was standing back in my bedroom door, so scared of what seemed to be unfolding before my eyes. Dad usually kept his rifle behind the door, but had been cleaning it, so it wasn't there. All he had for protection was the broom! Dad started reaching behind the door pretending to go for a gun and keeping an eye on them at the same time. At least that is what dad hoped it appeared to them. Dad threatened them that they better leave the porch immediately if they knew what was going to be good for them! Suddenly they took his threat seriously and left our porch so quickly that the one on crutches didn't even need them anymore! When dad called the area sheriff he learned that a car full of men from out of town stopped in Vernon and spread out all over town. The restaurant owner had already reported them and a state trooper had caught them before they fled town.

Looking back on this scene I shudder to think what would have happened to this little eight-year-old girl if God had not intervened in our behalf. I like to mentally see a band of angels rushing to our rescue just in time to fill those men with great fear. "The LORD is my rock, my fortress and my deliverer; my God is my rock, in whom I take refuge. He is my shield and the horn of my salvation my stronghold" (Psalms 13:2, NIV). **A rose.**

New Piano

During that summer there must have been some discussion about a new piano. One day men came to our house to move the old upright piano into a truck. My aunt had heard of a piano restoration that could make my piano look new. She provided the truck to haul it to Sandoval where that procedure began. It was called cutting it down. They didn't really cut it down. They simply cut out a section at the top and installed a mirror across the full length of the piano which made it look shorter. The large legs were very ornate and dust catchers. They were replaced by sleek slender legs. New ivories, newly finished black keys, and new varnish stain overall transformed my piano into looking brand new. It stayed my friend until a couple of years after we were married. **A rose.**

Business Venture Promotion

We finally got it all moved when the larger grocery store across the street needed some help in cleaning the dairy case and produce bins. I eagerly accepted the job and working after school and on Saturdays learned the difference between lettuce and cabbage. Lettuce is a lot messier than cabbage. Graduating to the meat counter, I learned how to recognize beef from pork. It's important to know these things, you know. But the log of chunk cheese was the hardest to guess what size of slice makes a pound! My first try on the electric saw produced a slice of two pounds and a half! The customer was cool with it. He laughed about it and bought it anyway. **A rose.**

The cash register was the most fun. I had to still count the purchase price out to the amount of money the customer gave me. It brought back memories of "Let's play grocery store, dad." The owner's wife was my seventh-grade teacher, and she taught me many things that gave me a "bird's eye view" of the grocery business. And then there was the gas pump out in front. I pumped gas for the grocery customers at thirty-five cents per gallon. Oh, for those days!

Explosion

The most unusual section of the store was in the very back. The owner was a skeet shooter and reloaded his shells with powder when there were lulls in business. In addition he was a smoker! Many friends warned him of this danger, but he disregarded all of them. One day there was a large boom and I had no doubt what had happened. I wasn't working that evening but lived across the street. As several of us ran over to see what was left of the store and owner, we found a rather humorous sight. His cigarette had dropped live ashes onto the light powder spilled on the floor and caught it on fire. The explosion threw him backwards onto the floor several feet away, singed all his eyebrows, burned his nose slightly, and broke his glasses! Otherwise he wasn't hurt, except maybe his pride. This miracle was added to another one in that his large container of powder was only a few feet away unopened. If the explosion had reached it there wouldn't be a grocery store or owner to tell the story.

Summer Project

During my high school freshman year the home economics teacher told us we could earn extra credit if we wanted to complete a project. I had been thinking about changing my bedroom to make it more colorful and airy. I wasn't interested in any cooking projects, but I did consider the prospect of decorating my room.

My grandma, who had all the baby animals recuperating behind the cookstove, had moved from the country into a little house in Vernon. She overheard the discussion concerning my summer project. She mentioned that if I was thinking about wallpapering my bedroom walls, she could teach me how to make wallpaper paste. It was available to purchase but if I could make it for free - why not? So I went to a wallpaper store and picked out paper for my walls. It was a white background with tiny orchid flowers scattered throughout. It made my room look so clean and bright. Grandma taught me how professional paper hangers cut multiple lengths at a time which made spreading the homemade paste over the backs much faster.

Home economics included sewing, so I decided to make new curtains. The easiest way I could think to do it was to purchase a bolt of white terry cloth and hem long lengths of it for curtains. For new bed dressings I bought a white chenille coverlet and white bed skirt which I dyed violet to match the tiny flowers on my wallpaper. Dad built strong sturdy shelves in front of my windows where I placed planted flowers when the winter dropped into temperatures too cold for the flower to survive. The last step was to clean and wax the floor. I was so proud of my room on which I did most of all the work. Needless to say I received an "A" for my project.

Revival Prophecy

An evangelist from Kentucky came to our little church to preach a revival. One of his introductory statements was, "I am new to everyone here and you are new to me. I might say some things in my messages that you don't agree with or understand. I suggest you take these messages like you eat chicken. Eat the meat and leave the bones on the shelf. God will enlighten them as needed."

Later in the week he called me up front to tell me he had a word from the Lord for me. I don't remember all the words except this: "God is going to use you in a music ministry and your music will be a blessing to thousands of people." Nothing more was said of it during the remainder of the services. I am not sure I heard the rest of it. It was something so out of the ordinary for me at that time. He didn't know me. Returning to my seat I immediately heard whispers from the enemy. "Yeah, right. So how do you think that can happen coming from a little town like this and in a tiny church? Where could you see that many people?" I just decided that I can't figure it all out. Either it will come to pass like he said, or he is not the man of God he represents. It is in God's hands either way. I can't do anything to change it or make it come to pass in my own strength. **A rose.**

High School Graduation

Meanwhile I was approaching my senior year of high school. The principal had retired and a new one was hired. Word had gotten out that my school had become rather hard to control. That was news to me, but he came in with the mindset of cracking down on all areas and making no exceptions.

Up to now I was carrying an A average in grades. I was exempt from taking the physical exercise class because of religious beliefs. The church which I had grown up in taught against the wearing of shorts. I went to an extra study hall during that time. The new principal refused to recognize this arrangement. He said it would not be allowed, plus, I couldn't graduate anyway, because I was three years short of attending that class. I had accumulated extra credits and only needed two more to graduate. I offered to take additional classes, but he was adamant that it would not be allowed. I asked again if my religious beliefs were not going to be upheld. His reply was negative. My parents didn't consider taking legal action, so I returned my books and left. The enemy tried to have a heyday with this. Tried to tell me I couldn't ever graduate, get a job, or amount to anything. "What are your friends going to say? Here you are Salutatorian of your class and can't even graduate. You will become a laughingstock in the community." My immediate prayer was, "So Lord, what do I do now? I am standing on my convictions and trusting you." **A broken sidewalk.**

Sunshine After Clouds

When we explained the situation to Aunt Woggie, she said, "I am so sorry. However, that's not a problem." When she started teaching they only required an eighth-grade diploma. After all those years teaching the laws changed, and she had to add a high school certificate to continue her teaching position. She enrolled in a correspondence program from the American School of Chicago and finished the four years equivalency by mail. So, you have probably guessed what opened up for me. She enrolled me in the same school, paid the tuition, and I received my high school diploma there as well. Praise the Lord! He promises to meet our needs! **A rose.**

Summer Employment

While I was working on my correspondence courses, the Lord opened several opportunities of employment there in our little town. I covered vacation time for the telephone operator. My dad played music in a little combo that comprised of himself, two brothers, and the circuit clerk of Marion County. The latter was a twin who was the president of the local bank. He hired me as a bank teller, and I worked there until his twin brother lured me away to Salem County courthouse to work there recording deeds and other official documents. Then he lost the election which made me available to switch to a lawyer's office to fill the secretary's position after she passed away.

My last position as a single person was field secretary for Mobile Pipeline Oil Company. It was a three-man office literally out in the oil field. I worked as receptionist, typist for the three men, and managed the switchboard duties. Oh, and the coffee! My office was where the boss and engineers would come for coffee which brewed all day long. It smelled so good that I finally overcame my distaste of this beverage and ended up actually liking coffee.

When I was offered this job I was reluctant to accept it because of the solitude of my surroundings, but the salary was so tempting! It topped everything I had done so far. Eventually I did, and that is where I saw again those switchboard lines needing to be plugged in and out. Memories come flooding back. Remember those nights of playing grocery store making change? Selling door-to-door giving me confidence of working with the public? The time when I was teaching myself how to type? God was truly blessing me way beyond what I could expect or imagine. The reference to the bump in the road of not graduating now reminds me of the scripture in Genesis 50:20 (NIV) where Joseph was reassuring his brothers of being forgiven of their treatment to him – "You meant it for harm, but the Lord intended it for good to accomplish what is now being done." This scripture is what I joyfully threw back into the enemy's face. **A rose.**

Southern Gospel Music

I was heading in a new direction for now. Ever since I was a little girl I had heard music of somebody called the Blackwoods Quartet. My parents usually went to Vandalia to shop on Saturday nights. On the way home dad would turn on the car radio and we would listen to the Blackwoods. I didn't know anything about who they were or how much they would influence my love of that style of gospel music. As time went on and I was working in various kinds of employment I found a music store which carried records of many different gospel quartets. Every week I would check them out for new recordings to purchase. I became hooked on this music and bought myself a stereo to listen to them. I listened to it over and over every night after work. My interest developed to even desiring to accompany a quartet in that field.

Early in my teenage years I told the Lord I was happy being single. He had blessed me with a good job and my own car. I was teaching piano on the side and playing for church. My parents would love for me to live with them forever. Even rent free! I had a close friend who sang and also played accordion. We did duets or I would accompany her on solos. By the way, this gave me an opportunity to learn how to accompany. It requires a different style of skill than solo performance. I didn't know how much I would appreciate it later on accompanying for a quartet. **A rose.**

My List

In reference to the possibility of marriage it made me sad to see friends who rushed into relationships which ended in divorce, leaving them in a life which became difficult to navigate. Especially with a new little one to support and care for all alone. It was definitely not what their dream had been. Nor was it mine. So I reminded God that IF he ever sent someone to cross my path I might consider it, as long as he met the following requirements. Imagine me telling the Lord how to bow to my requests! Playing piano for a gospel quartet had been developing into a very strong desire. On my list for a future mate were these qualifications: 1. Had to be a Christian. 2. Had to be involved in music ministry of some kind, preferably gospel quartets. 3. No more than five years older than me. 4. Being handsome and kind would be a definite asset if you want to throw that in as well! After all, doesn't the Bible tell us in Matthew 7:7, "Ask and it will be given to you; seek and you will find; knock and the door will be open to you?"

At some point I was relating these requirements to my grandma. Her eyes began to twinkle as she replied that when the love bug bites I will forget everything I said. Well, my quick response to that was, "Oh no, grandma, I know what I want!" Do you know what God did? He was so merciful, gracious, generous, and humorous! It was as if He went down the line and started checking every one of those things right off my list! Almost all. Tom is six years older than me! God has a sense of humor and let me know He was still in control for what was best for me. Earlier at a brief time of feeling discouraged before this all took place, God allowed me to have a dream in which I saw a vague figure of Tom's build and dark hair. His face, though, was not recognizable. My faith in God rose again to total trust and belief. **A rose.**

My Dream Came True

I had actually seen him once at a local concert where his quartet was singing. However, I didn't get to meet him afterwards, because my girlfriend's high heel broke off going down the steps and we had to go home. I had been attending several other gospel concerts where each one left me yearning more and more to be playing for a group. Several quartet groups were booked in the Centralia High School for what they used to call an all-night gospel sing. Slowly over the years the length of these concerts shortened to end around 11:00 or so. The Envoys Quartet was on the program and doing their introductions. I learned that their pianist was leaving for college and they would soon be without a musician. Adding to that their bass singer was single and very handsome. My heart began beating faster by now! I began praying, "God, can this possibly be your promise coming true for me?" I didn't know how close I was to having my prayer answered. **A rose.**

I can't remember much else about that concert. At the end I walked back to their record table hoping to meet him, which I had never before had the nerve to do. Instead their lead singer, who was also single, decided I was there to talk to him. Now what am I going to do? It seemed forever before Tom got back to the table from tearing down their equipment. It suddenly dawned on me that the longer the lead guy talked the better chance there was of the bass singer getting to their table. In my mind I was silently praying, "Please keep talking!" Tom finally got there and after introducing himself invited me to come back the next Sunday afternoon to hear their concert which was close to our area. My life was soon to experience God's providing the most exciting time of living my dream and watching God doing an incredible answer to prayers. **A rose.**

A Whirlwind Courtship

That second time of going to hear the Envoys Quartet outside on the courthouse lawn marked the beginning of a whirlwind courtship. The Envoys Quartet had planned a picnic July 4, 1966, at the Greenville park, so Tom drove to Vernon to pick me up. He didn't know at the time, but dad was very impressed with Tom that first day of meeting him. Dad was sitting outside in our swing by the door. Before Tom came inside to get me he sat down with dad and took time to talk. Dad never forgot the respect Tom showed him. One hurdle passed! **A rose.**

Another time was when we were already engaged. We were looking for a refrigerator for the home Tom had found for us to rent. After looking at what our budget needed to be, he decided maybe we should play it safe and go with a used one until we had a better handle of the checkbook-to-be. Dad saw wisdom again in Tom's careful decisions. Dad was hooked on his little girl's man.

Parental Approval

Before leaving, Tom came in and spent time with mom talking and laughing with her. She approved of his Christian character, gracious manners, and sense of humor. Later his praise of her good cooking gained him very high points with her as well. We were well on our way with approving parents! **A rose.**

Our weekends after the picnic were spent with me driving to hear their concert or him driving to Vernon where I lived. I was twenty-two and he was twenty-eight. Our relationship quickly became serious. In later years he said he was running out of all his savings driving back and forth that far! Also, he would quip that when he found out I could play the piano, that sealed the deal. He figured out he better marry me while I was available! Men are so matter-of-fact! Of course, he was much more romantic when sharing his thoughts with me! **A rose.**

My Engagement

August 17, 1966, I was staying at my grandmother's house in Patoka where I had attended high school. The country roads had been freshly oiled and I didn't want to drive on it with my new car. This afternoon when he drove down for the weekend he took me by surprise.

On Bended Knee

He asked me to join him outside. I sat down on her swing in the yard. Waiting in suspense, he knelt down before me on one knee and asked me if I would marry him. The realization flashed through my mind, "He is proposing to me!" It didn't take long to answer, "I would love to." I was thinking *oh, my! This is really quick!* But I reassured myself that we will have time to get to know each other a lot better in the next year or so. I had often dreamed of being engaged for a couple of years before getting married. During that time we could do some traveling and really get to know each other.

Reflection on Similarities

Seriously, each of us had been believing for a long time that God had one special person saved just for each other. Praying for guidance, each of us had a peace within our spirits. We had so much in common. We were both

Christians and had been involved in gospel music. He had a natural gift for art. Mine was instrumental music. My Aunt Woggie majored in art and taught it in first and second grades. Both our parents were German/Irish. His parents were six years apart with birthdays on June 30 and July 3. Our birthdays were six years apart on July 19 and 22. Our fathers both worked on the railroad. Both our mothers were excellent cooks and bakers. I think Tom got the lesser benefit from that one, since I didn't think I would ever be interested in cooking. I remember thinking, *Oh, my goodness. I can't even have a grilled cheese sandwich without making it myself!*

  I was quickly gaining more appreciation of my mom's spoiling me with her copious cooking skills. Time did make a change in that area though. I quickly worked on culinary skills.

Length of Engagement

  Later when we were discussing when we might want to get married I suggested maybe next year, perhaps in June 1967. Don't all girls dream of June weddings? He didn't understand the year thing. His idea was 1966! It took me a while to process all this sudden information. However, I quickly readjusted. December was out of the question because that was Christmas and I didn't want to mix the two. That backed us up to the month of November which was as close as we could both agree on. Many people since have asked us if we told our daughters this was okay for them too. Absolutely not!

Setting The Date

We both had full time jobs. Tom worked at Olin Corporation as an engineer, and I was working for Magnolia Pipe Line as field secretary and switchboard operator. We both had our new cars. So November 19, 1966, became our special day! To this day I am so grateful for God's promise of Psalms 32:8 that says, "I will instruct you and teach you in the way you should go; I will counsel you and watch over you." **A rose.**

Wedding Plans

With the wedding date set there was a flurry of things to be done. Fortunately where I worked, a bakery provided the cake, punch, mints, and nuts. An engagement photo was needed. Flowers were chosen and being brought by the caterer. My colors for the fall wedding were gold, orange, and green. After getting assurance from my maid of honor and bride's maids they could be available I found the right color of material for each of their dresses and turned it over to them to have them made. Their white satin shoes were sprayed to match. Special friends from school gladly served at the guest book, serving tables of cake and punch, as well as at the gift table. The rest of it was my job. I still loved to sew so I found a picture out of the Aldens catalog of a wedding dress I liked and found material in a fabric store right at home in Vernon. Many evenings I spent at the sewing machine working on my dress. It was finished just a week before the day we got married. My mother's dress and my veil were turned over to another seamstress in town since I didn't have time to do it all. Through all these busy, busy days I felt like I was dreaming. It was coming together like a miracle. God was surely shining His love and blessings on us!

Wedding Day

Meanwhile, Tom had been looking for an apartment to rent since he had been living in a small apartment. Also he had to find his groomsmen. He invited his college friend to be his best man. The friend's darling little girl became our flower girl. She was so cute! Tom's groomsmen were the tenor and baritone members of the Envoys Quartet, and our vocalist was the lead singer. Of course all the guys had to be fitted for the shirts, shoes, and tuxes. I wonder if he realized how much work was involved in planning the wedding! Eventually God helped us get everything all ready.

I felt like the heavens opened up with special gifts for our wedding day. We got married on a Saturday at the Overland Pentecost Church in St. Louis. The weather was fantastic that day. Not a cloud in the sky. I was familiar with this church because I had been there several times participating in the music for their rotating fellowship meetings. The church was beautiful, with red carpeting and an organ. Evidently, I was thinking about the effect for pictures. The little church I attended in Vernon didn't have an organ and would have been too small for the ceremony. Tom didn't have a home church at that time since he was traveling weekends singing in the Envoys Quartet. I had become acquainted with a young girl during those fellowship meetings and learned that her father was a photographer. The Lord was orchestrating every step just as it should be! **A rose.**

The Ceremony

The ceremony went as planned. The ushers brought our guests, grandparents, and parents to their seats, and the attendants made it down the aisle as practiced with help from the music of the organist. Dad was so proud as he accompanied me to the altar. Preceding the wedding he gave me a good luck penny to put in my shoe. I saved that penny for years before it somehow disappeared. I can almost taste the beautiful cake today. The very top of it was an open bible made of sugar. It is safely stored today fifty-seven years later in our freezer. When the pastor said a prayer for us Tom reached out and held my hand. That was so sweet and very touching.

The Honeymoon

We spent our honeymoon first in Kentucky where we visited the Happy Goodmans' church. Then on to the sandy beaches and brief daily rains of Florida. On the way home we drove back to Vernon. Dad had driven my car there from the wedding. So we picked up the car and the wedding gifts we had received. Later, we celebrated our one-year anniversary at that same hotel in the same room.

Our First Home

Oh, how we enjoyed our first little four-room house in Wood River. I remember thinking while sweeping our porch and sidewalk, *I am sweeping the steps and sidewalk of my own house! I live here!* I just stood there momentarily thanking the Lord for all His blessings. Quartet practice began in the dining room. My piano had been moved there from Vernon. I was somewhat nervous the first time, not really knowing what style they expected me to play. After a few rehearsals and hints that I wasn't playing loudly enough I learned to play much louder. I had forgotten that in performances they were going to be on microphones and they needed me with no mic to be loud enough for them to hear. I soon got the hang of it. My dream was coming true. **A rose.**

After several concerts we learned that our first bundle of joy was joining us. Some of my family thought I would have to stop traveling on the road when that baby got here. They hadn't figured it out that God would provide for those extra needs as well. And that was exactly what He did. When asked what I would do with our son while I played the piano, I explained that if the church didn't have a nursery I would pick a sweet grandmother-looking soul and ask her if she would like to hold him while we sang. As it turned out, they usually responded with pleasure. Other times the church's nursery came to our rescue!

Several years later this cute little boy tried several musical instruments in school until he eventually discovered singing. There was no question when he was coming into the subdivision. You could hear him singing in the car with the stereo as loud as possible and all the windows down and even over the lawn mower. He later became the lead singer in our family group and with his wife blessed us with a grandson and now a great granddaughter. **A rose.**

Our first little home was very sufficient for us except for the fact it was on a busy highway. Noisy trucks rolled through at all times of the day and night. People threw trash out the window which caused us to have to pick it all up before we could even mow. A couple of days after we brought our newborn son home my husband called to say he was going to pick me up and show me a new house he found in Godfrey. I wasn't in too great a shape to go sightseeing, but I thought that if he wanted me to see this now it must be very important to him. He was so considerate and thoughtful of me. Well, I fell in love with the house immediately. Our parents came up and helped us pack and move the next day. We rented this house on contract for deed for two years. **A rose.**

When the two years were up there were too many things we would like to change. My husband was blessed with experience in blueprints and artistic drawings and we agreed, "Why not?" He can make the drawings for the way we want it and start new. Every night after work and dinner he would retire into the basement at his drawing board and create drawings for our new home.

At first, I said I wasn't interested in seeing it being built. I would wait until it was all finished and then I would go over to check it out. But curiosity got the better of me and I found myself wanting to see what progress was being done. Our little boy was able to sit up in a wagon, so I would put him in the little wagon and pull him to our street daily. It was exciting! When they were measuring where each of the walls would be on the floor I panicked thinking the rooms were so tiny they would not be big enough to hold our bedroom furniture. My husband reassured me that they would appear much larger when everything was finished. It would be okay, and, as usual, he was right. Our son now had a larger nursery for his very own room.

Second Bundle of Joy

Our excitement of moving into our beautiful home that my talented husband designed was heightened by the news of a second bundle of joy. She made her announcement of future arrival on the same day we moved in our new home. Several months later we were blessed with a blond, blue-eyed daughter. She was quite the opposite in personality from her brother. Very quiet, easy to please. She would even prefer us to lay her down to sleep rather than all that rocking!

As she grew older she developed a great talent in art and poetry. Having a quiet, sensitive nature she also reached out with a mega love for all animals. Several years later she blessed us with our first two grandsons and now two great-grandsons. **A rose.**

During her younger years she was responsible for a long list of animals becoming members of our family. There were dogs, cats, a turtle, canary, and even a guinea pig. I am probably leaving out many others. Actually anything with legs, fur, or feathers qualified. Today she still has a special little dog who thinks he is a person! One cat in particular will be etched forever in our memory. Like all cats, she loved being as high up as possible. One year at Christmas time we had a short Christmas tree on a stand between the living room and kitchen. I think she was heading for the top of the refrigerator, not quite sure. Anyway she took off, and the Christmas tree was evidently in her way. She made a flying leap right into it and through the middle of the tree much to our amazement. I don't remember any broken ornaments in the process, either.

As the cat grew older it became heavier. She had her favorite places to nap. Actually she would sleep anywhere. We still laugh about when she was sound asleep on the arm of the couch and fell into the waste can. Talk about speedy scrambling for safety.

Cat's retirement years crept up on her, and she became very portly (fat is more like it). About twenty plus pounds worth of it! She moved rather slowly and blended well with the color of the living room carpet. When piano students came she felt it was her duty to check them out and did so. My husband was embarrassed one time when she refused to leave them alone. He picked her up and took her back to our younger daughter's room. Rather irritated he hurled her into the room. However, he didn't take into consideration that her door was closed. She didn't reappear for a long time! **Not a rose.**

I think that the cat got even with us. She had learned that if she jumped up on the bathroom sink there might be a possibility of drinking from a dripping faucet. One Sunday afternoon we were resting from our morning concert and I went to wash my hands. My wedding rings were on the sink after the last time I washed my hands when I didn't put them back on. To my horror they were not to be seen.

My husband even took the plumbing apart thinking he could retrieve them. No rings. I now wear a different set of wedding rings. Still don't like cats. **A broken sidewalk.** When my honey replaced them he blessed me with even larger ones! **A rose.**

Our third bundle of joy

Our third bundle of joy was a second son. He was so cute, mischievous, a leader of his friends, and the owner of odd parts of bicycles and skateboards for several years. Some of my husband's tools disappeared every once in a while, too.

As he grew older he sang and played drums for us. Since his room was in the basement his drums shared the room with him. Those beautiful musical booms of rhythm came through our floors for a long time. He was dedicated to practice, that was for sure! People would ask us how we managed the noise. We said that wasn't noise to us. It was music to our ears. We appreciated his enjoyment of a musical instrument, and we knew where he was. We were so proud of his many talents. We watched how he turned a one-hundred-year-old house into a beautiful home. He now is an excellent drummer and restorer of vintage drum sets to original condition. After being blessed with a total of seven grandsons from our other children, he and his wife gave us our first granddaughter, plus two more grandsons. **A rose.**

A Parent's Nightmare

He gave us a horrible scare when he was two years old. My mom was in the hospital and we were on our way to visit her. On our way we stopped at her house and fixed lunch for us and my dad. Our young son had full range of grandma's country house as usual. When it was time to eat he was fussy so we let him lay down to take a nap first and decided he could eat right before we left for the hospital. I looked around to see if he might have found some candy or other treats which could have spoiled his appetite but only found the cat's dish which had remnants of cooked eggs. When I picked him up he was as limp as a rag doll. I didn't want to frighten my dad and didn't mention anything but told my husband that something was wrong with our son. He quickly got the other kids together and hurried to our car. **A broken sidewalk.**

By the time we drove down their country lane our son was trying to cry but it sounded as if he was in a deep, deep well. Not much sound was audible. We stopped the car so I could get him from the little bed in the back of the car and hold him. With him now in my arms we started again, his eyes rolled back into his head, he went limp, and no more response was visible. My husband drove way over the speed limit hoping for a state trooper to escort us to the hospital. It was about twenty-five miles away. But no troopers. I began to pray. I declared by faith over our baby that he was just unconscious and had not breathed his last breath. *Please, Jesus, I am trusting You to keep him until we can get to the hospital.*

Upon arrival at the emergency entrance I remember rushing in ahead of everyone else and told the first nurse in the hall to please take him quickly, he is not responding. She rushed into the examining room. Doctors and nurses came running from all directions to help. My husband and our other two children came in, and he called his parents to please drive to Centralia and take them home with them for us. A doctor came out of the examination room and asked me if he had eaten anything that could have been poisonous. I related the only thing that I was aware of, thus, the eggs in the cat's dish. He asked me to call my dad to have him look around the house for anything that he could have gotten into. Any open bottles, jars, etc. Another nurse came out and told us they had pumped his stomach and found a large number of pills. My dad looked and found a new box of my mom's blood pressure medication. Back then medical pills were still being dispensed in paper boxes, not child-proof containers. Dad thought he had searched the house thoroughly for anything that might cause a problem before we got there. This pill box was in her nightstand pushed way back out of dad's sight but perfect sight for our son's height. It turned out that he had eaten the whole box except for a few which he had licked the color off of and dropped the empty box on the floor.

The Diagnosis

My husband was downstairs waiting for his parents to come for the other children. The doctors now knew what the problem was. They called me into their office to explain the severity of what just happened and to prepare me for the outcome. They explained that no adult could swallow that many of those pills and survive. Our son is only two years old and even if he lived he would only be a vegetable. His kidneys would not function, he would be unable to talk, walk, or move on his own. They gently told me I wouldn't want our son to have to live that way. I was hearing what they were telling me, but I was mentally calling on God's help. Suddenly I felt faith building up in my spirit. "And we know that in all things God works for the good of those who love him" (Romans 8:28). "Jesus looks at them and said, 'With man this is impossible, but not with God" (Mark 10:27). "All things are possible to them that believe" (Mark 9:23). I respectfully responded to the doctors that I knew they were telling me what it looked like in the medical field, but we believe in prayer and we also believe in miracles. We had many people joining us and believing in God answering our prayer. The doctors were polite but I could tell they thought I was just hoping in vain.

Somehow, I had found time to call back home to the church where we were booked to sing that Sunday night. I explained that we were in a Centralia hospital and our son wasn't expected to live. I also called our home church in St. Louis. They both went to pray for us. Later our home church said they called as many members as they could and they all prayed until they felt a peace when they knew that God was doing a miracle.

A Brand-New Machine

The hospital auxiliary had just purchased a machine that could monitor many things at the same time, and our son was the first one hooked up to it. It was moved outside the nurses' station and continually provided heart, breathing, and multiple other readings all Sunday night, Monday, and into Tuesday. His heart would register dangerously low and then race to over 200 beats per minute. My husband and I took turns talking to him all night. The nurses said if he ever became semi-conscious maybe our voice would help him become more conscious. On my husband's watch our son's heart stopped two times. You could hear that machine beep all over the hospital. I immediately woke up and ran back to his crib. Constantly praying and talking to our son as though he could hear us. If we ventured out of his room for any reason, everyone knew about our son. They would come up to us and ask if we were the parents of the little boy who ate his grandma's medicine. They would go on and let us know that they were all praying for us.

Our Miracle

On Tuesday morning I was on watch when his eyes opened. He looked at me and said "Mommy!" He was talking and saying words that he knew! I checked his diaper and it was wet. His kidneys were working! Nurses came running with the news. The doctors checked him over and couldn't find anything wrong with him. By afternoon he was dismissed to go home. One of the nuns in this Catholic hospital said to me, "I wouldn't have given a copper penny for his life when he came in." Miracles still happen today! Pray for yours and believe! **A very broken sidewalk to a beautiful rose.**

Tri-County Christian Bookstore

While we were traveling through Illinois, Missouri, and Iowa we were working days at Tri-County Bible Bookstore in Brighton, Illinois. Tom had been looking through the ads and found a Bible bookstore for sale. We talked about it and decided we were interested. We purchased this store in 1975, and I worked there during the days.

We offered Sunday School and Vacation Bible School materials for churches, music, books, Bibles, and relevant Christian items. There were also opportunities for piano and guitar lessons. One of my former piano students taught beginning piano and another friend taught guitar. Tom was working full-time as a design engineer but came in after work and weekends to help with building new book shelving and arranging the inventory to keep it looking fresh if we weren't singing somewhere. There was a room in the back which we made into a mini-kitchen-play-room-nap area for our three kids. During school months many homework assignments were completed there.

Our third child, a son, at this time was about four years old. He was quite mischievous but also very charming. He soon became a favorite of the customers as he tried to memorize their names. All three of them rode their three-wheelers back and forth to the gas station to buy snacks and candy. They were always looking for dropped change to see who could find it more quickly. During a snowstorm Tom accidentally lost his key ring. He offered a monetary reward to whomever could find it. The older two about ran over their brother trying to get out to the snow drifts first. But he was the one who found it buried in the snow. Money talks! The other two got mad at him saying, "No wonder. That's not fair! He was the closest to the ground!" As if that made any difference! **Still a rose**.

Blessing Bundle #4

When we brought her home we thought we finally had a dark-haired baby girl. But the black hair began to disappear and was replaced with one more baby girl with blond hair and blue eyes. She, too, responded quickly to music. When she first sang a solo she had to stand on a milk crate to reach the microphone! At home she kind of ran the household. We found out she a calendar in her room keeping track of our appointments! Later in life she went into medicine and became a passionate nurse, plus blessed us with five beautiful grandchildren! Four boys and a daughter. **A rose.**

When this fourth baby was known to be on the way, Tom decided that traveling weekends, running a Bible bookstore, and adding a new baby was too much to do by myself. We advertised it for sale and two couples joined forces, purchased it, and moved it to Godfrey, Illinois. So it continued to serve the community with Christian materials. **A rose.**

Recording Studios

To further the ministry we were able to produce several records. CDs and DVDs hadn't been available yet. Our favorite recording studio was in Flora, Illinois where we recorded four albums. Our fifth one was in Nashville, Tennessee. That one was rather difficult for me. My grandmother's funeral was held the day before we left to record. Many prayers followed us and gave us the peace we needed to focus on the music.

Radio Program

God blessed us with a weekly radio program on KXEN 1010 on the dial in St. Louis where we played our recordings and stories of our travels. We even got an opportunity for a few appearances on some others' TV programs. The greatest blessings came from seeing souls giving their heart to the Lord and experiencing the joy and blessings that are available to them forever while serving Him the rest of their life. **A rose.**

Classroom Music

Having four children added to our family made it very expensive to enroll them all in Christian School. So I traded my music skills for free tuition in Beltline Christian School the school-year of 1982-83. At the end of that first year in the classroom teaching I felt that I owed them certified music instructor credentials. Meanwhile I learned that one of my friends had enrolled in Lewis and Clark Community College. She and I shared piano skills at our church. That encouraged me to take the plunge and complete the studies.

Lewis and Clark Community College

Our oldest son was shocked that his mother was going back to college at my age. He said to me one day that I was going to be the oldest student on campus! I reminded him that he should visit the college again to see the large percentage of older students studying for or adding to new degrees for occupational changes. He was graduating early from Alton High School and pre-registered for LCCC, so he and I did homework together at the kitchen table and on the bus traveling to our concerts on the weekends.

My two years at Lewis and Clark Community College were 1983-84 at the age of forty-two. I enjoyed every minute there. The campus was beautiful and the music staff were so helpful and friendly. New experiences opened up for me, like tutoring theory students, playing piano in the pit for the musical "Dolls and Guys," Student Senate Representative for the Music Club, and serving as president of Student Senate later in the following semester.

One Christmas, I experienced one of the most painful

falls I ever had. As usual I was in too big of a hurry going down our basement steps and not holding on to the banister. The basement family room was dark as my husband and son were watching tv like in the movies where all the lights are turned off. Only the light from the tv screen offered any direction. I turned to see what channel they were watching. As I turned, thinking I was now on the bottom of the basement floor, I discovered I was in the air missing the last three steps. I quickly turned back to grab the handrail but in doing so I fell on the steps with my foot under me and twisted my right foot completely around to the back. That resulted in my losing about three months of mobility. The ankle had been broken into three pieces. Now I was the owner of two rods and six screws holding my ankle in some semblance of original shape. **A broken ankle not a sidewalk.**

When I was able to return to teaching my classes, the music building was newly constructed with an elevator to the lower level. My husband would get me and my wheelchair into the elevator and go to the lower lever for classes. Whichever student wheeled me to a different classroom got an "A" for the day. **A rose.**

Several weeks went by and I had now graduated to crutches. I hobbled to the stage during a student recital. I was supposed to accompany a vocal major but couldn't use my right foot yet to manage the damper pedal. So I turned to the right on the bench a little and pedaled with my left foot. It felt weird but it accomplished the job. Coming down from the stage I heard a lady say, "Did you see her pedal with her left foot? They sure do teach strange things here today!"

Well, I didn't stop to explain; it worked! **A rose.**

What is Music Therapy?

It was at Lewis and Clark Community College that I first heard of Music Therapy. All the music majors were in a Music Educators National Convention meeting. Our chapter sponsor mentioned that there was something new in the music field called Music Therapy. He didn't have a lot of information yet for us so he told us if we were interested we would have to research it on our own. It sounded interesting to me, but I had all I could handle at the moment trying to study, practice, and travel on the road with a family. I put it out of my mind. But God was working His plan.

Southern Illinois University, Edwardsville

Goodbye, Lewis and Clark Community College and hello, Southern Illinois University. Two years after earning an associates of arts degree, I transferred to Southern Illinois University, Edwardsville for my bachelor's degree in music education.

Senior Recital

At the end of my studies at SIUE I was required to present my senior piano recital. Playing a piece from each of the four periods of music history turned out to include 25-plus pages of memorized music! By now, playing for the quartet concerts, I was comfortable performing before audiences of all sizes. But accompanying singers is a completely different story from doing solo playing. When accompanying you feel like you are kind of safe in the background. Being out front with the lights on only you was a totally different world. Then adding in the memorization factor of all those pages was enough to put a person over the edge. It took months of learning the music and finally the memorization.

Four weeks before the final day of recital it was customary to perform one of the four pieces each week before the whole department of music majors. The requirement was intended to give the student practice in performing in front of an audience. I told myself *I can do that.* Easier said than done!

Recital Practice Procedure

The day came for my first piece to play in the SIUE concert hall. I bravely stepped out and did very well until a moment of brain freeze! *No problem*, I said to my myself. I jumped back to the beginning and started over. Well, when

I got to the same place, guess what! Yes, you guessed it. I couldn't think of what was next. I knew the material, had worked for months, and could perform it well at home and during lesson times. In fact, my husband had heard the material so many times he could tell when a mistake was made.

Reality quickly set in. There was a great possibility that it could happen on the day of recital. The kindergarten students where I anticipated teaching didn't know or care how well I could remember Bach, Beethoven, or Brahms. They probably would gladly choose "Twinkle, Twinkle, Little Star" but the university was very much concerned that I did. In fact I either remembered it and performed it well or my diploma wouldn't be awarded! **A broken sidewalk.**

Once again I presented my problem to the only One who had solutions for me. "Please, Lord, I need wisdom to know how to proceed and finish my requirements. You helped me all the way to this goal, and I know you will help me over this last hurdle." Philippians 1:6 (NIV) promises: "being confident of this, that he who began a good work in you will carry it on to completion until the day of Christ Jesus." I felt the question arise, "Why don't you ask for permission to change the venue from the recital hall at the university to your church? You are very comfortable playing there, it's close to the university, they have a Kawaii grand piano, and there will be a large group of praying friends backing you up."

The possibility of this solution began a wave of relief welling up. At the same time my heart began to beat wildly because it had never been done that way before. With one last reasoning of "I'm not a Music Performance major, I am a Music Education major," I presented my case to the instructors involved and went out into the hall to await their decision. It seemed to stretch out for an eternity! I wanted to see the doorknob turn, but I also dreaded to hear it turn. Finally it turned. With sweaty hands I jumped up to hear the verdict. My piano instructor said, "They granted your request!" PRAISE THE LORD! **A rose.**

A Broken Piano String

The Wednesday before my recital on Sunday our church had invited a well-known gospel music musician to share his compositions. He had written many beautiful pieces, had a heavy touch on the keys, and during the concert had broken a string in the piano. I didn't know this until the next day. Panic set in again, and I asked, "What are we going to do now?" We only had three days until that Sunday. The date had been set and invitations and been sent out. The tuner came and said he could put in a generic string, but because there isn't time to order an original one from the factory it wouldn't sound exactly as the original. By now I was in the mindset of "Let's just do what we have to do and get it finished."

Recital Day

Sunday came. The weather was beautiful, and the church began to fill up. Our chiropractor's family came in and walked to the front row. His wife told me later that they told their three boys that they were going to sit up close to me, be praying for me to be able to relax while playing, and if they so much as sneezed to distract me they were dead meat! A little rough sounding, but the boys got the message! I stayed in the choir room waiting for the time I was to walk out. I kept telling myself, "I am going out there to practice one more time."

One hour later I bowed for the last time, thinking, *Thank you, Jesus! Only you could have gotten me through this with not a single forgotten note!* All those prayers, all those hours and months practicing and memorizing all those pages of music. Three professors from SIUE, who were the ones grading my program, left positive comments on their sheets. Their only negative was, "It would have been nice if the church would have had the piano tuned!" I, too, could hear that generic string every time I needed it. But I just put it out of my mind and stayed focused toward the last note to be played. I never told them why there was one string that really didn't belong in there. I was too happy now for it to make any difference. This served as a reminder in many times of struggling that if He can help me with that, there's nothing He can't get me through with His help. **A rose.**

A Bird's Eye of Worship

Meanwhile our quartet concerts took us to many different styles of worshipping churches. It allowed us to be appreciative of how God works in different ways His wonders to perform. It was such a blessing having our children travel with us. As time went on they joined us with just our own singing family. One of them was very quiet and shy so she decided that wasn't for her. She gave it a try but said there were too many faces watching her, so she was content to join the congregation during concerts. We traveled and sang weekend to weekend, in all kinds of weather, to share our music. We wanted to encourage others with what God had done for us and what He wants to do for them.

Only A Milkshake

One of our concerts ended with a very frightening experience. We had left a service with the spirit moving in a mighty way. On the way home we stopped at a three-way red light. The truck behind us failed to do the same and slammed our van into the car ahead of us. The driver had just purchased a new truck and had left a fast-food place with a sandwich and milkshake. Reaching down for another drink he failed to notice that the lights turned red. **A broken sidewalk.**

We had our four children, a friend of our son's, and all

our equipment in the van. My husband and I were thrown backwards into van, throwing our glasses into the back. Tom's seat was bent all the way back. He was able to exit the van and raced back to the truck to see what had happened. Seeing the frothy bubbles on the driver's face made him think the driver had been drinking. He found out it was only a milkshake. The driver was very apologetic and offered his help. Our girls were crying and I started praying for our health and safety. My husband and I found our glasses back in the van totally unharmed. Someone came from a restaurant across the street and took the girls over to get them a drink.

When we were checked out at the hospital the doctor thought our oldest daughter had a spinal fracture, but tests later didn't support that assessment. No one suffered major injury except for a cut on our younger son's head. Inspecting our van the next day we realized what a miracle it was. Even after the van was towed away we saw our four microphone stands still standing upright across the middle of the van appearing to have prevented the heavy equipment from sliding toward the front! They could have been like arrows piercing many of us all in front of the van.

We lost track of the older couple in front of us. Their car didn't have much damage from our van being pushed forward into them. I pray the lord restored any loss they may have experienced. I wish I could have seen into the spiritual realm that day to see how many ministering angels were there for our benefit! "Because he loves me," says the Lord, "I will rescue him; I will protect him, for he acknowledges my name. He will call upon me, and I will answer him; I will be with him in trouble, I will deliver him and honor him. With long life will I satisfy him and show him my salvation" (Psalms 91:14-16). **A rose.**

Overnight Snowstorm

Our Iowa programs seemed to always end with snowstorms. One in particular just had light snow when we arrived for a Saturday night program. As is the case many times when the church is a long distance from home, they would either place us in a member's home for the night or book us into a motel. This time we left with a family after the program and followed them way into the country to their beautiful home. I am sure they didn't realized it, but they took us to our bedroom which had no heat. It was freezing cold! At that time we had our son and infant daughter with us. To keep her warm we took her out of her portable crib and placed her in bed with us. I think our son curled up at the foot of the bed. I am sure no one even wiggled during the night! A blizzard had developed during the night and dumped about three feet of snow. They were used to this type of weather and had a tractor ready to break a path from their home into town for their Sunday morning program. The home owner lost his muffler trying to get out of his driveway. I kept wondering what we would do if we met another vehicle. The path was only wide enough for our van. The Lord kept it open all the way to the church.

Boy, did we appreciate the warmth inside the church that morning! Both of our kids developed colds that weekend, but we had a wonderful service. **A rose.**

Surprise Visitor

Our singing group went through several name changes. As members changed it became a trio, back to quartet, to a two-family group, and finally our family, "The Singing Houcks."

For a while we were traveling as a two-family group in a motor home which was wonderful during the day, but there wasn't enough room for both families to sleep at night. So our families took turns going to a motel. One night when it was our family's turn to sleep in the motor home we had just settled down for a good night's rest. The concert was over and we were tired because we had traveled a long way to get there. I was already asleep when my husband heard some commotion outside around our vehicle. Tom peeked out the curtain and saw two young men siphoning our gas from the tank. They had assumed we were sleeping in the motel which would leave the motor home open prey for some free gas. Tom banged on the door and yelled as angrily as he could to go away. The two men looked up so shocked to learn that there was someone in there, and it scared them out of their wits. They didn't even take time to take any of their tools or gas can with them. They took off running as fast as they could go, jumped over (or into) a muddy ditch, and that was the last we ever saw of them! **A rose.**

Want Some Gum?

We experienced some other humorous times as well. Churches would usually provide a potluck dinner after the service or bless us with going out to a restaurant. At this particular church we were standing in line for the food to be ready, and a lady came over to us and was commenting to us what a cute toddler we had. I had just noticed how much gum someone in the nursery had given him. In the process of saying how he needed to spit it out she reached out her hand to shake hands with Tom, and our son removed his wad of gum and placed it in her hand. She looked at the present in her hand and appeared so bewildered as if to say, "Oh my. What do I do with this!" We were just as shocked as she was. Quickly we recovered our embarrassment, apologized, and retrieved the gum. She probably walked away thinking, "Maybe he isn't as cute as I thought."

I'll Pass

My dad learned to play many stringed instruments during his life after learning his first one, the violin. When our daughter decided to play viola in her school orchestra he was thrilled. As she grew more proficient on it we began adding her solos in our concerts. If we were singing anywhere close to where dad lived he would always join us there and bring his violin. His favorite hymn was "Whispering Hope." One Sunday we were booked to sing in Centralia, Illinois. Dad was excited to get to play this hymn with her. They played their duet and did a great job as usual. After that, the pastor took up an offering which gave us a break to catch our breath. I thought I had caught a whiff from dad's breath but didn't dwell on it very long. As the offering plate came down our row where we were sitting, dad took one look at it and announced, "No thanks. Don't believe I care for any!" And passed it on down the row. It was all I could do to squelch not only my giggles but those of each our kids.

Job Opportunities

Upon graduation from SIUE I was offered a part-time job as a music instructor for fifth and sixth grade classrooms. I was appreciative of this immediate opportunity so soon after graduation. I didn't realize it would contain a large part of teaching vocal music. There were two large choirs involved. I felt like it was way outside my ability and interest. **A broken sidewalk..**

Further into the semester I was talking with the Lord about this and explained to him I would love to have a music teaching position more from a keyboard and theory angle than general music. Little did I know how soon that position would come my way.

My phone rang and the voice on the other end was a longtime friend who also was involved in teaching piano. It had been some time since we talked so I didn't know she was working in a program called Preparatory Music Program. There were several college music instructors offering music lessons for students of different ages and skill levels on various instruments. Lewis and Clark Community College was offering this as a service for the area. Its purpose was to help prepare young children for college music classes later. My friend organized their teaching schedules as well as preparing regular recitals of the instructors' students in the Chapel.

Toward the end of our conversation she informed me that she was resigning from this job for family reasons. Then she remarked that they would be looking for a replacement and suggested I apply for the job. She even recommended applying that very same day as she thought someone else was wanting the job.

What a chunk of sudden information! I had to stop and

try to process what I had just heard. Actually that job would basically be the same thing I had been doing over the years of private piano lessons. Just in a larger scale. Once again it was like the Lord checked off everything on my list. He had been preparing me for this all along. The opportunity was now open if I would walk through the doors. It seemed as if he had tailor-made the job and requirements for everything I had asked of him. I am so thankful for Psalms 37:4 that says, "Take delight in the Lord, and he will give you the desires of your heart" (NIV).

I took her advice, drove to the college, and applied. The Dean of the Music Department remembered me as a student in his classes from two years prior. Walking back to my car I felt like I was walking on air. The position started immediately. This was so enjoyable, getting acquainted with the numerous instructors and their students. I was allowed to my bring my personal piano students to be included in the programs. It was time for the quarterly recitals. Plans were already in the works, including three recitals. It took that many to present all the students enrolled in the Preparatory Program. Additional teaching opportunities were given me along the way, adding college Piano Classes I and II, Basic Music Theory, Theory I and II, and Applied Music Students. I was living my educational dream. **A rose.**

Students of Blessings

During the years of teaching piano I made an attempt

to keep track of all the students' names and years when we worked together. But teaching two semesters per year for several years at Lewis and Clark Community College made that impossible. However there will always be a student here and there who stands out in your memory.

One such student had signed up for Piano Class I. As she progressed through the semester I was noticing how easily she sightread her music. In casual conversations I learned that she was single and had been involved in music for quite some time. Every once in a while my handbell choir needed a fill-in to ring. So one day after class I approached this student and asked if she had ever had the opportunity to ring handbells. Her face lit up and said she did not but would love to learn. It didn't take long for her to get the hang of it. By a few months she was able to hold two bells in each hand, thus being able to read four notes at one time. She became one of my most advanced ringers who covered many a different spot in the choir. Not only that, several years later, we have become best friends. **A rose.**

Another student walked into my room asking if it was the piano class. I reassured her that she was in the correct room. Her smile and demeanor told me that we would somewhere get to know each other a lot better. Her smile just lit up the whole room and portrayed a person who surely loved the Lord. Weeks later into the semester I learned that she composed vocal pieces and enrolled in my class in order to learn how to notate them on staff paper. She had a beautiful voice which she shared with her church and in the community. She composed a new piece of music for each of the classes she attended. Our keyboard class was blessed with a piece of hers entitled, "Better, You're Getting Better." She shared that the title and melody came to her early in the morning after talking to the Lord about how difficult it was to count out the rhythm for class and in her compositions. I now hold digital recordings of her awesome vocal range and original pieces. Another friend for life. **A rose.**

I always felt honored to stand in class and reach out to future musicians with genuine interest and desire to help. Being in a secular college meant religious beliefs were not to be discussed in class. But they all knew that my office was always open if anyone wished to drop by to visit or share any concerns. **A rose.**

Even my private piano students gave me some interesting experiences. A family of gymnastics trainers enrolled their sons for lessons. It came time for a first lesson for one of the younger ones. My doorbell rang, and I went to open the door. Suddenly I was taken back with the thought, "What was that blur that just went past me?" That cute little red headed freckled-faced bundle of energy just completed three handsprings across my living room! Never touched a thing in the process. He landed on his feet and looked very impish as he grinned and said, "Hi."

The next week I thought he would come in with a little more traditional entry. He has been here once and knows my house and where the piano room is. Wrong! I opened the door and repeat of last week. I didn't say anything to him but I was thinking, "I am going to be ready for you next week." Before opening the door I positioned myself in front of his path and immediately pointed out where he could hang his coat behind the door. Problem solved! The scene rescinded to memorable events. I never told his mother until years later!

So many memories of piano students over the years! God gives you the opportunity to watch them grow up in your weekly time with them. They quickly become members of your family. I humbly thank Him for His blessings and pray that I can be a light that shines with Jesus' love.

A long time ago, a Christian family enrolled their adopted daughter in piano with me. There were several lessons until she got brave enough to give me a smile or initiate dialogue. At first I could barely hear her "Hi" or even see her turn toward me and look into my eyes. Of course, I didn't know anything about her background, so I had to pray that God would give me wisdom to gently give her love and a feeling of a safe and secure place during music. As years went by she began to open up like a flower. I felt like I was watching a little bud finally gain strength to expand into whom God had planned. She remained very quiet and had a sweet spirit, but would now share questions and issues. She grew up and blessed me with becoming a babysitter for us. She blessed me again with the opportunity to be the pianist at her wedding. After the wedding she became the pianist for her church. Later her adoptive mother shared with me that her daughter talked with me about her problems more than with her. I can't take credit for that. That is all praise to our heavenly Father. **A rose.**

Handbells

My precious life-long friend, benefactor, teacher of nature, Aunt ("Woggie") Elta, was fading in health. She had to be hospitalized several times before being transferred to a nursing home. Soon after her death I purchased three octaves of handbells. With the initial purchase there was a memory bell included. I requested the inscription of "In remembrance of Aunt Elta Peyton" and her date of death. She had supported every single part of my music background, so I wanted to show my appreciation by dedicating these bells to her. I had been attending workshops learning the basics and found them to be very fascinating. The bells and the beautiful chordal accompaniments echoed up into the ceiling as they were played. Several of the church members volunteered to practice with me until we were ready to do our first program. Our group's name became Riverbend Ringers. Many organizations used "Riverbend" as part of their name since Alton is located in the bend of the Mississippi River.

In the beginning only three or four of thirteen ringers that was needed to ring three octaves could read music. To make it easy to learn initially I had them color their right-hand notes green and their left-hand notes pink to identify when to ring. But they soon caught on to the techniques needed to read music. Many of our programs were in nursing homes, schools, and churches, as well as outdoor events.

We played primarily folk, sacred, and songs from musicals to spread the Good News and encourage people in their walk with God. In order to lighten up the music of sacred, folk, and gospel music one of the ringers was a registered Christian Clown. Proverbs 17:22 (KJV) says, "A merry heart doeth good like a medicine." She dressed in clown outfits, and entertained the audience with her ridiculous faces, props, and playing her notes incorrectly on purpose. Other times she would lay down her bells and without notice would just walk off into the audience to start talking to someone. Messing up the song was one of her special tricks! The audience loved it. **A rose.**

One time our clown found a long director's baton and painted the handle bright red. She pre-warned the girls that when she raises the baton they should all start playing. I was facing the audience introducing the next song. She interrupts saying, "I want to direct this piece." I exclaimed she can't do that because she doesn't know how. After bantering back and forth she wanted to prove that she could. Our clown being rather tall climbed up on the stool I usually sat on, and raised her hands with her baton. As the girls started to play, the clown's baton went straight through the ceiling and got stuck in it. That was even more hilarious than she had planned!

During another program the theme for the day was family. I was talking to the audience about how important family is to all of us. Our clown had sauntered off and stopped at a lady's chair. With one arm around the lady the clown started waving her other arm with huge gestures, interrupting me as usual. Finally I addressed her only to be told she had found her aunt. "You didn't tell me you had an aunt here!" "Oh, I do. I can prove it," she said as she reached down and pulled a large metal shape of a black ant from under the lady's chair! I never knew what she was going to do next. But she really brought a lot of laughter and merriment to all who were there.

Along with the humorous elements there were testimonies of God meeting needs of others. One of my ringers just recently shared with me how playing the handbells helped her to reconnect with God in a very real and personal walk with Him. Up to that point she never experienced people who talked positively to her or gave her due credit for her abilities. She was literally at the point of giving up. She even had it planned. One night a snowstorm had developed during one of our concerts, and I was afraid for her to drive thirty-two miles back home in the dark. I invited her to spend the night with me and my husband so she could go home in daylight. She couldn't understand why someone would invite a total stranger into their home. She said that was the starting point of her breaking down the walls she had built around her heart. A few months later we were playing for the opening of our Christmas Program. I invited her to stay for the remainder of the service. The church musicians were playing, "Shout to the Lord." The Holy Spirit tugged at her heart until she re-dedicated her heart and life to the service for the Lord. She even got re-baptized!

A year later she left home very early for a concert and was on her way when she hit a deer. I was desperate for a fill-in ringer so I quickly drove to retrieve her and we both got back just in time for our concert! She realized then how important her part was and how much we depended on her to be there. At another time we were blessed by her arrangement on clarinet of a Christmas carol which was added to our program. How great is our God! She claims I pushed her out of her comfort zone, but it was really the Lord! **A rose.**

Center Cemetery

My dad's side of the family had their own family gravesite that went way back in history. It was a cemetery called Center Cemetery surrounding the little church that most of them attended. All the members of the family involved pitched in down through the years to pool enough money for its upkeep. As years went by the members slowly decreased in number. Along with decreased numbers contributing to the expense the amount of money also decreased. By the time it came down to me there was very little money left in the fund. My Aunt Woggie was the last family member to be laid to rest there. My parents and my husband and I had chosen other gravesites for our immediate family. That left us with a cemetery with no one interested in it and no money left to keep it maintained. Plus, I now lived ninety miles away and couldn't check on somebody mowing it and keeping its appearance respectable. **A cracked sidewalk.**

I prayed for God to help us know what to do about this. Out of the blue my phone rang one day with a gentleman asking if this was the owner of the Center Cemetery between Augsburg and St. Peter, Illinois. Wondering how he found me, I answered that I was. He introduced himself as a member representing the Mennonite families who had been moving into that area from Pennsylvania. They had enough requirements completed for a new community to the satisfaction of their headquarters except for one thing. They had no location designated as their burial grounds. He wondered if my people would be willing to share our cemetery. In turn for this consideration they offered to maintain all of it at no cost to us. It didn't take me long to answer in the affirmative! To make it legal, both parties drove to the courthouse and obtained a document stating our agreement and sealed it with a one-dollar charge. Which I gladly donated! We have returned a few times since, and they have kept their word in maintaining the cemetery in immaculate condition. God is definitely concerned about our daily needs and provides answers to our prayers! **A rose.**

Italy Concerts

Let's return to some exciting developments with playing handbells. The Lord just dropped a blessing into our laps! I had barely gotten my feet wet directing the Riverbend Ringers when a good friend of ours offered Tom and me an opportunity of a lifetime. Being a music educator in our area, he had been taking his handbell choir on educational European trips performing about every 3-4 years. In 1998 they had been planning a trip to Italy when one of his ringers dropped out because of sickness in their family.

He called to ask if I might be interested in filling in for the missing two handbells. I couldn't believe my ears!

Tom and I never considered any overseas traveling. We had no idea how to navigate those myriad types of details by ourselves. After a short-very short-discussion we decided we would love to go with them. Serious practicing got underway. It took many hours of rehearsal to become sufficiently comfortable. Each ringer has to hold a bell in each hand representing two different musical pitches. Example: E in the left hand and F in the right hand. You would think with my playing and teaching piano and reading music all those years that by now it would be a piece of cake! Wrong! Adding to that is the fact that playing the bells takes different skills than directing them. Wow, when I went back to rehearsing with my handbell choir I had a much better appreciation of what they were having to learn. But he and all his ringers were all very friendly and helpful to me in this new adventure. I still really appreciate all their understanding, friendships, and opportunities which allowed us such a time of enjoyment and learning. **A rose.**

Germany Concerts

2004 found Tom and me considering another overseas trip to Germany. This again was with the same handbell group with whom we traveled to Italy. There were two vacancies for other friends, so we had the privilege of inviting a couple friends of ours who had recently gotten married. Germany is my heritage country on my grandmother's side, as well as Tom's dad's side. We felt as though we were traveling back in time visiting home!

The city streets were very narrow, so our bus had to park several blocks away from the cathedrals where the concerts were to be. We soon realized that pack mules would have been a blessing from above! All the equipment for five octaves of bells, hand chimes, tables, covers, music and music stands, cases, and costumes had to be hand carried for blocks! Tom didn't realize he would become a pack mule! We were fortunate to have so many strong and willing men to accommodate the task. They were affectionally called our roadies!

Concerts were traditionally scheduled later in the evening. That was different than here in the states. I had a pleasant surprise when a close friend walked in for our first concert. She, her sister, and mother had been previous piano students of mine who lived only one street from our house. She had graduated from college and moved to Germany, but I was not aware of it. What a small world!

Cheryl Houck

Several concerts, whirlwind shopping times, and visiting surrounding cities later produced a group of close, happy, weary friends ready to return home. We had experienced awesome foods, friendly people, and beautiful cathedrals in which we could listen to the bell tones float all the way to the top of ancient ceilings! There are many warm memories that we still enjoy today. **A rose.**

Silver Anniversary

What beautiful memories we have of our 25th anniversary! We are so blessed! All four of our children stood up with us for the repeat of our wedding vows. I wore the same wedding dress that I made twenty five years ago (only let out the seams a "little" bit!), and dad's penny went back into my shoe just like before. Our oldest son sang a solo for us, and our youngest son wrote a beautiful poem and painted it on a special plaque for us. One of my young outstanding piano students played the organ wedding music for us. Even the sugar figurine in the shape of an open Bible came out of our freezer and was placed on top of the cake. All of them surprised us with a limousine ride from the church to the German 518 South Restaurant in Jerseyville, Illinois. We will never forget how much they contributed to our enjoyment and feeling of pride for them all. They made it so special for us! **A rose.**

Master's Musicians

Somewhere in the middle of 2007 I was sitting in the congregation at Abundant Life Church enjoying the worship. We were blessed with enough musicians in the church to take turns with playing for the Sunday morning services. Today was my day to not play. I was thinking how wonderful it was to not have to be concerned about what song was next, what tempo, or what key it was written in. No sooner did that thought go through my head than another voice interrupted, "Yes, but how about the small, maybe storefront church who only has one musician and she wakes up in the middle of Saturday night running a high fever? What do they do? Who can they call to cover the music at the last moment?" Wow, I never thought about that. What do they do? Wouldn't it be nice if there was a central number the pastor or music director could contact at the last minute? Could I perhaps put something together for that purpose?

I probably never heard another word of the pastor's

sermon. My mind was racing toward what would it take to accomplish this goal. I am involved with several different musicians on a daily basis. Some of them are college students, some are retired musicians, and there are some of my own students who might qualify. Immediately I started contacting those who I thought might be interested. Fortunately, the list was longer than I expected. But what could we call this voluntary group of men and women musicians?

Our church ladies were getting ready for a Women's Retreat in Branson, Missouri. In the bus on the way to Branson I was sharing the need for a name for this group that was forming. At the time the only thing I was thinking was something about M&M's. But that was candy! That wouldn't work. The retreat was very refreshing and uplifting. On the way home it popped into my mind. The M&M's could represent Master's Musicians! How exciting it was watching how God revealed a name so fitting. **A rose.**

What an honor it was to be able at a moment's notice to help out with a church's music. Many times it was an occasion where vacation notices could be planned ahead of time. At other times it was the urgent last-minute type of call. Letters were sent out to all local churches detailing what was available. In the beginning we asked for an offering to cover gas and advertising expenses, but it eventually evolved into accepting whatever the church's budget was. It became a service that was very helpful to the church as well as the musician. **A rose.**

Unfortunately, the list of volunteers has dwindled over the years to a skeleton crew who is still active. Organists now are very hard to find, almost like a needle in a haystack. Many churches have abandoned organs, and replaced pianos with keyboards. Worship teams with string instruments have been popular for several years. Also, young people are not readily choosing sacred music studies for an occupation or even vocation. But perhaps music is like other areas; arts, fashion, architecture, and standards which will make the full circle back. Many churches are still struggling in their searches for musicians. Hopefully the trend of sacred and gospel music will soon return with new and even more ways to worship our Maker.

The OK Kids Music Club

The Abundant Life Church was forming activities for different age groups. Clubs were popping up with things of children's interests. I thought, it's time to bring back the bells. Only this time they won't be gold, they will be multicolored. Why not a kids' bell choir? Someone had already chosen a name for them, "The Overflow Kids." So we called ours "The OK Kids Music Club" for children ages five through eleven.

Each of the handbells was small for the little kids hand strength. The bells were a different color, each representing a letter of the music scale, A,B,C,D,E,F,G. I grouped them in sufficient colors to spell a chord. There were three major groups. Then as they sang the song, I would direct them by which group was to ring the same time as a guitar would be chording a song and providing the foundational music. They wore the traditional white gloves just like the adult handbell choirs. During their performances they also shared their music with percussion, strings, and keyboard. Occasionally, a puppet would sneak into the program! Matching shirts were provided with their club's name. They were so cute! People in nursing homes, assisted living places, and church enjoyed the little ones singing and playing for Jesus! A rose.

Later on the Abundant Life Church was again looking for additional things for the children to do, which opened up an opportunity for some children's music. There was a supple inventory of modern kids' songs and videos, but they needed some of what I call our heritage group of kids' Bible songs. The church ordered some CDs of those songs like, Jesus Loves Me, The B-I-B-L-E, Hide It Under a Bushel, It's Bubbling, It's Bubbling, Climb Up Sunshine Mountain, and many others. After starting these songs in the classrooms on Wednesday evenings a mother was walking down the corridor exclaiming how wonderful it was to hear those songs again. She came all the way into our class to say how happy she was to hear they are singing them once again! **A rose.**

Volunteer Time

A few years had flown by since graduating from SIUE, subbing in the Alton School District as music teacher, and enjoying several years at Lewis and Clark Community College. I often thought back to that time of my life of teaching piano, music theory, and coordinating the Music Preparatory Program. Tom had retired from his design engineering position and I decided it was also time for me to retire and enjoy being at home together.

Alton Memorial Hospital was looking for more volunteers to answer the telephones. By now our youngest daughter was working there as a registered nurse, and I guess I thought it would feel like I was working there, too. Besides, it was something new and different from anything I had ever done. It dawned on me that if I was going to be able to answer the phone or direct visitors to offices or patient rooms I needed to learn where they were all located. Delivering mail seemed to be the very thing that would provide the training. I asked if that would be available and it started me on my time spent there as a volunteer. Eventually I returned to my original goal of answering the phones. Even now I look back on those days with warm memories. It allowed me to meet many friends, give an encouraging word, and become a better informed volunteer. Little did I know how much I would later appreciate this overall knowledge of the hospital's layout. Unbeknown to me, the Lord was preparing me for the next new chapter in my life. **A rose.**

Music Therapy

Early in the morning, around an unearthly time to be awake, I woke up completely awake around 3:00 am. I never wake up this early! It was like I had never gone to bed. My brain was trying to figure out why I was awake. That in itself is somewhat of a miracle since when my head hits the pillow I'm out. Immediately. Even storms and sick babies don't disturb my sleep. When our kids were infants Tom had to shake me awake to take care of them. He laughs about all the times he would be talking to me only to find out I was sound asleep.

The room was so quiet! It was hard to describe. Perhaps a reverence of someone in the room and an expectation of something to come. Did Tom wake me up? I looked over at him and he never moved a muscle. I sensed a presence which brought me back to the moment. I said, "Lord, this has to be You. If you are trying to tell me something, I am listening." Immediately it seemed as if a voice was talking, not really, but my brain was translating it into recognizable data. "Remember something called music therapy?" Instantly my mind went back in time to when our students' music sponsor was saying in our meeting that there was something new in the field for music majors called music therapy. However he didn't know much about it yet, so if any of us was interested we would have to do our own research to learn about it. But as the old saying goes, it went in one ear, and out the other. There was too much going on to start something new. I was taking college classes, singing and playing gospel music with my family on weekends, doing homework on our bus, and tending to home and family affairs all at the same time. Research? Whew! Please!!! Totally out of my mind. So I thought.

"Lord, if You want me to do something with this, You will have to throw me some rope of information. I don't know what it is, where to find it, or anyone who might be working in this field. Characteristically, I don't normally jump off cliffs without knowing where I might land, so I want you to put someone who knows in my path so I can talk to them." I was also hoping He still had a sense of humor. After all, He did have the audacity to wake me up at 3:00 am! **A broken sidewalk**?

A week later I was answering phones at Alton Memorial Hospital. One of the directors walked over with a couple of boxes of envelopes and letters that needed to be folded, stuffed, and mailed out. He explained that his secretary was swamped with other pressing duties and couldn't finish these letters completely in time for the mail. Could I possibly help? I readily agreed to do it because there were a lot of times I sat there waiting for the phone to ring and had nothing to do. How I hate to be bored!

I folded and folded and folded in between phone calls. After some time I became curious. Wonder what was in those letters? I picked up one of them to read it. The hospital was sending out an informational letter informing the community what services were now available at Alton Memorial Hospital. Well, what do you know! There was a gentleman's picture at the bottom of the page, and under his name were the initials, B.C.M.T. Board Certified Music Therapist!!

I couldn't believe my eyes! "Lord, do you mean there was a real music therapist right here under my nose, so to speak?" My heart was beating a lot more beats now per minute than normal. "I don't know him or where he is, so, Lord, I want You to cause that man to walk past my desk sometime so I can talk to him. I've got a lot of questions!" Still on a broken piece of sidewalk.

The desk at that time was by the Beeby Wing elevator. Visitors were entering and leaving that elevator which caused me to look up repeatably. All the way down the hall a man was turning the corner and heading towards my desk. I was thinking *he looks a lot like that man's picture in that flyer I was folding for the mailing.* The closer he came the more I was convinced it was he. When he was close enough to speak I reached up and removed the receiver from the phone's base and placed it in my lap. I couldn't afford to let this opportunity slip through my fingers simply because of this phone ringing! Sorry, Lord. I will ask Your forgiveness afterwards!

Here I go, Lord! "Excuse me, sir. Are you by any chance a music therapist?" He responded yes, he was. "Do you have a few minutes to talk? I might be interested in whatever that is." He was so polite and informative. As it turned out he was a board certified music therapist, minister of the gospel, retired music teacher, excellent organist, and professor at the Maryville University! All wrapped up in one person. God surely knows how to provide our needs! He invited me to visit his class on a Friday afternoon. His class provided active music therapists who came and described their field of music therapy. It was wonderful receiving a bird's eye view of different areas of music therapy. **A rose.**

I was hooked! It really spoke to my heart as an area I could serve the Lord with a genuine love for the people and being able to base it on music. My mom used to visit nursing homes and read scriptures to them or wrote letters for them. She always took me with her. Sometimes I would stay outside and play with my dolls or at other times would take my accordion inside and play music for them. I had developed a fondness for the older population. They take you just as you are and are not critical. They reach out for love and friendship with an eagerness to share their experiences. Older people are so appreciative of every tiny gift of assistance. If you observe them closely you can see the little girl or boy of yesteryear peeking through.

Enrolling at Maryville University

All this new information was coming forth right as the fall classes were forming at Maryville University. The gentleman standing at my desk didn't know if there was enough room for one more student, so he called the Dean of Music Therapy and asked her to please hold the last opening for the fall class because he had just met someone who was serious about enrolling. He made an appointment for me with her in order to fill out the enrollment papers. She was very gracious in helping me choose the proper classes to fulfill my goal for the next two years. She even found another student living close by me who agreed to carpool with me from Godfrey to Maryville. **A rose.**

Audition

In this meeting she mentioned I would have to prepare an audition for acceptance. Oh my, nothing was said to prepare me for that again! My stomach did a couple flip-flops thinking about it. There wasn't enough time to prepare anything classical. When she saw the startled look on my face she told me not to worry about it. She knew I played for churches and improvised musically when playing for our quartet. So, she suggested I play something like what I would do for an offertory or for our group. Whew!!! What a relief! That audition was so easy compared to the senior recital I had to perform for graduation. What I didn't know was the gentleman who was the epitome for excellence in piano performance was supposed to be in that audition but had to be out of town that day. Two gracious professors were the only ones present, and they both made me feel very comfortable. **A rose.**

Completing Three Practicums

The classes were very intense but so enlightening for me. I looked forward to each and every day. I was continually blown away in learning how powerful music can be for any disability. In addition to the classes we had to fulfill three practicums. That was where we got hands on experience. The first one was working with a class of many young people with different disabilities using different techniques. The second one was teaching and directing a geriatric choral choir at the same site as the whole practicum using handbells. The third one was using handbells again but driving to different sites throughout the length of the last practicum.

Internship

Now it was time to be accepted for an internship for approximately six months. I was granted permission to spend my internship with geriatric hospice. Part of it was working out in the field, and the latter part at the Alton

Memorial Hospital.

The clients in the field were home-bound, so we drove to their house. I will never forget one of the occasions working with a client in the field. They were way out in the corn fields. My supervisor pre-warned me to not be surprised when we went in, because they had six dogs all inside. How could you do anything musically with that many dogs barking? He suggested to wait and watch how they all had their favorite place once the music started. He sat down and opened his keyboard. One of the dogs placed its head on his arm as if to get as close to the music as possible! The others went different directions as if they had been assigned their place and appeared to announce, "Okay, we are ready." He started playing the keyboard and within ten minutes all six dogs were asleep! I could hardly believe my eyes. Music is powerful for both man and animals. Humans are hard-wired to respond to music. It soothes, relaxes, and opens memory for those who otherwise can't even say their name. During the right selection of music the client can sing every word from way back in their memory. Then when the music stops they slip back into their other world. When in low- and moderate-intensity of exercise, music can override signals to stop. Thus you can continue for a longer period of time. When in pain the music helps redirect the brain from the discomforts to music which is more pleasurable. We are told that music stimulates more parts of the brain than any other human function. What a gift God gave to mankind when He created music! **A rose.**

Alton Memorial Hospice

The portion of my internship at the hospital was very rewarding and interesting. I placed my keyboard on one of the rolling carts and went from room to room offering music to the patients. Often I would get a request to go to their special room for hospice patients. One of these visits was completed with my thinking why did this young man seem familiar to me? The nurses told me he was very agitated and unable to relax and it was too soon for more medication. I started the session, and his parents came in to visit. While the soft music was continuing his father called his name and said, "Listen to that song. It is your favorite hymn." The patient started to lay more quietly and became more relaxed. I didn't recognize him yet because his father called him by his full name. Later that evening it came back to me. I had him in music class while at Beltline Christian School and knew him by his nickname. I was so thankful for the opportunity to be with him at this period in his life. I enjoyed offering him music when he was little, and was now so thankful to be able to minister in this latter portion of his life with his favorite subject, music. Thank you, Lord! **A rose.**

My Motto

I spent more time in regular patient rooms than in the hospice room. During my time taking music to many patients I was thinking about all the painful procedures that they endured and multiple shots piercing their skin. When I was interviewed for a press release I mentioned that my motto was, "When music hits, it doesn't hurt!" Hopefully the music helped divert their focus from the pain and discomfort to something more pleasing.

Documentation

I was required to record the clients' heart rate and breathing rate before a music session, during the session, and again after the music session. Their numbers at the end of session usually measured approximately 15-20 points lower. When the breathing and heart rate lowers, the client benefits from less anxiety, more relaxation, and improved mental outlook. When that happens they are more receptive to benefits from their medication and nutrition. The best compliment the music therapist can receive is when the patient goes to sleep in the middle of the session!

Directing In Mid-air

One of my clients after graduation was one of the sweetest ladies I have ever met. Her daughters, knowing how much she enjoyed music, asked me if I would provide music therapy for her. It was a pleasure. She was always happy, smiling, and eager to please. A beautiful Christian lady! Later I learned she, too, had been a music teacher and therapist! When it became time to transfer into hospice care I received a call from her daughters saying that their mother didn't have much time left and could I please come back. I had been there just the day before. When I arrived their mother appeared so peaceful and non-responsive. As I began softly playing her favorite hymns, she began fidgeting with the covers. It bothered me wondering if I was playing the wrong song or too loud? As I continued playing and observing her she finally got her arms out from under the covers. I will never forget what happened next. She managed to raise her right hand over the covers and moved it in the air as if she was directing the hymn for a choir to sing. Exactly on time with the hymn I was playing! I motioned to her daughters to watch. All three of us were in tears and speechless! I felt that she was assuring us that she knew we were there and that she was okay. Our loved ones can still hear in their last moments. She left this world doing what she enjoyed her whole life. Directing and sharing her gift of music. She graduated to her heavenly choir soon after I left her room. Incredible! **A rose.**

I purposely chose the geriatric population and hospice for my special study. Many people have commented to me how depressing that age group must be knowing that their days are numbered, and will be here no more. My response has always been, "It is not depressing for me because this is how I feel. When a person reaches the point in life that the doctors have done all they can do medically, there is still an opportunity to reach out to them with love and comfort. I can't give them anything else. Not books to read, not new clothes, special gifts, boxes of candy, nor taking them on trips to other locations. But I can offer them music." We are taught that the hearing is the last of the senses to go. They may not be able to respond to music with words or movements but they can still hear it.

50th Wedding Anniversary

How exciting! We reached our 50th wedding anniversary! It didn't seem real that we had been married that many years. You don't think about a 50th wedding anniversary when as a young couple you walked down the wedding aisle. All of life is in front of you. You race through those first years, enjoying being newlyweds. God blessed us with four beautiful children. You don't see any of the difficult times ahead. Praise the Lord, He plans it that way. But oh my, He sure makes Himself instantly available to help us navigate through the rough waters. Fifty years of looking back over our shoulder gives us documented evidence that all things are possible with God. Blessings, healings, miracles, protection, love, mercy, and the list goes on and on. There is no other way to spend your life on your own and experience all the blessings He has shown us. God is an awesome God! The joys are immeasurable! The rough spots are made smoother and the burdens are make lighter. Only God can do that for all of us. At this point we had grown to a family of four children, twelve grandchildren, and three great grandchildren. This picture is such a marvelous testimony of a wonderful life serving God, especially for me growing up as a single child. Did I say, "God is a good God?"

Cheryl Houck

Covid Pandemic

When the covid pandemic occurred I had been playing piano for the seniors' services on Wednesday mornings. They preferred the older hymns so I would choose a special offertory each week based on that style of music. However, when the pandemic started our church doors closed to public services and the seniors couldn't come to their special service to worship with their favorite songs. Because we were also between children's pastors I had been telling Bible stories for the OK kids at our church and putting them out on YouTube. I asked myself, "Why can't I do those offertories the same way?" I felt sorry for the older people who couldn't get out to places for enjoyment of their choice of music.

Returning To Research

During this same time I had become interested in researching the background stories of how these hymns had been written. It is humorous now as I remember telling my professor in Music Therapy Research that if I ever completed my research paper I was done with researching and never wanted to research anything again! Famous last words! The Lord knew what I would find calling my name. Here I am eagerly looking forward each week to a new hymn with its history! He makes the road more smooth and our path more straight. **A rose.**

Recording CDs and DVDs

I continued for two years, researching the histories of hymns with the stories behind them. Up until now the only way I could share them publicly was to upload them onto Facebook and YouTube. People started asking me if I had ever recorded them on any CDs or DVDs. I was hoping to be able to do that but I didn't know how to do it, nor anyone who could do that for me. Once again I asked the Lord for help in accomplishing this.

After her lesson, I mentioned it to one of my piano student's mother. She immediately told me she knew someone who did that for her church and other people. God provided the open door once again to complete His plan for this music. I have shared them at our seniors' services, flea markets, and various venues. **A rose.**

Those hymns with stories are continuing each week first for the Seniors' Services offertories on Wednesdays and then the next day on Facebook and YouTube. I have received testimonies and notes from all over expressing appreciation for these hymns being shared. I look back over the years and can see how God was leading me in so many different ways to share His word in music. I am so thankful for all the opportunities He sent me. He gently led me out of my timidity to talk about His love and mercy. The time spent in music therapy has also richly blessed me in my work with piano students and mutual friendships. Through it all God has been so good all my life in providing all my needs, protection, and a life full of hope and enrichment in good times as well as difficult ones.

God Continues With A Hand of Protection

Tom and I were returning from a doctor's appointment on the interstate. He accidentally cut in front of another driver. They glanced over at him and did not appear very happy nor understanding. A little further down the highway the same car passed us. Suddenly a force hit our car on the driver's side so hard that it rocked our car. Thinking we had been shot I instinctively looked at Tom expecting to see blood running. My mind immediately was whirling, wondering how I was going to get our car off the interstate and get help for Tom.

He looked at me asking, "What was that?" There was no apparent injury. Our car continued down the interstate. By now we were really in shock trying to figure out what hit us. We took the first exit and traveled to a safe place to pull over. We got out of the car and checked for damages to our car. To our utter amazement there was no evidence of anything that had ever happened! Not one scratch! All we can say is how we appreciate God's mighty hand of protection! We are reminded of Psalms 32:7, "You are my hiding place; you will protect me from trouble and surround me with songs of deliverance. Selah." **A rose.**

Conclusion

Thanks to everyone who has read this far. I pray that you love Him and walk with Him. Proverbs 3:5-6 (NIV) says, "Trust in the Lord with all your heart, and lean not on your own understanding. In all your ways acknowledge him and he will make your path straight." He is no respecter of persons. He wants to walk with you, too, through your roses and broken sidewalks! I have to smile and tell God, "I can't begin to thank you and praise you enough!" As I am writing the last few lines of my musical journey for now I am listening to the song being played on YouTube, "Great Is Thy Faithfulness." **A rose.**

Epilogue

As I sat writing these words, God reminded me once again of His love for me and of His healing power. A couple weeks ago I had an annual physical. Everything came back with perfect readings included blood pressure, sugar levels, and cholesterol. Two nights ago my blood pressure suddenly spiked very high and I was rushed to the Emergency Room. One of our church's staff members rushed there and stayed a long time after praying for me. The tests started with my body shaking like a leaf, pain in the right side of my neck, and the inability to hold my right arm or leg up longer that a count to two or three. A CRT, two MRIs, and blood labs were taken. One by one each came back with negative responses. By the end of the next day they could only assume it had been a TIA, or mild stroke. There was not a trace of anything left to show what might have caused it or any trace of resulting damage. It was God's healing and erasing of all the evidence that could have given this story a different ending. This story started when God breathed life into my body. His presence and mercy has continued to cover me every day, enabling me to serve Him. Now at the end of this story He is still reminding me of His healing power and presence. He has never left me nor changed. He is the same yesterday, today, and forever! All praise and glory belongs to Him! John 3:16

says, "For God so loved the world that He gave his one and only one Son that whoever believes in him shall not perish but have eternal life." Now it is time to press on and reach out to new heights, new territories, and sharing the Good News! "Let us not become weary in doing good, for at the proper time we will reap a harvest if we do not give up" (Galatians 6:9, NIV). Amen. **A beautiful rose.**

About the Author

Cheryl Houck holds two bachelor's degrees in music education and music therapy. She taught for several years at the Lewis and Clark Community College in Godfrey, Illinois, and still teaches in her home studio as private piano instructor. Her family singing group, The Singing Houcks, has traveled many miles sharing their faith and music for different denominations. She directed the Riverbend Ringers Handbell Choir in local area assistant living facilities, churches, and schools. Her videos with background histories of the hymns are available on CDs and DVDs. Today she provides weekly music for churches and continues preparing weekly videos for hymns and their stories on Facebook and YouTube. Cheryl is married to Tom Houck and they have four children, twelve grandchildren, and three great grandchildren.

Printed in the USA
CPSIA information can be obtained
at www.ICGtesting.com
JSHW060820270823
47205JS00006B/11